T0360621

Regulating Open Banking

FinTech transformations have brought changes to the global financial markets and merit the attention of financial regulators across jurisdictions.

This book is one of the first ones of its kind to look at open banking (OB). It examines regulatory approaches to OB by taking a broad view of comparative legal systems and through perspectives of transaction costs, public choice, and institutional design.

The book looks at the legal implications by engaging in a two-tiered comparative analysis: comparing between compulsory and voluntary approaches to OB policies and comparing the legal systems between the West (i.e., the EU and the UK) and an Asian economy (i.e., Taiwan).

Chang-Hsien Tsai is Professor of Law and Business, Director of Institute of Law for Science and Technology, and Director of Master Program of Health Policy and Business Administration (HBA), College of Technology Management, National Tsing Hua University, Taiwan.

Kuan-Jung Peng is currently a PhD candidate at the European Doctorate in Law & Economics (Erasmus University Rotterdam, the Netherlands; University of Hamburg, Germany; University of Bologna, Italy).

Routledge Research in Finance and Banking Law

For more information about this series, please visit: www.routledge.com/
Routledge-Research-in-Finance-and-Banking-Law/book-series/
FINANCIALLAW

Regulating Open Banking

Comparative Analysis of the EU,
the UK and Taiwan

**Chang-Hsien Tsai and
Kuan-Jung Peng**

Routledge
Taylor & Francis Group

LONDON AND NEW YORK

First published 2023
by Routledge
4 Park Square, Milton Park, Abingdon, Oxon OX14 4RN

and by Routledge
605 Third Avenue, New York, NY 10158

Routledge is an imprint of the Taylor & Francis Group, an informa business

© 2023 Chang-Hsien Tsai and Kuan-Jung Peng

British Library Cataloguing-in-Publication Data
A catalogue record for this book is available from the British Library

Library of Congress Cataloging-in-Publication Data
Names: Tsai, Chang-hsien (Law professor) author. |
   Peng, Kuan-Jung, author.
Title: Regulating open banking : comparative analysis of the EU,
   the UK and Taiwan / Chang-Hsien Tsai and Kuan-Jung Peng.
Description: First Edition. | New York, NY : Routledge, 2023. |
   Series: Routledge research in finance and banking law |
   Includes bibliographical references and index.
Identifiers: LCCN 2022040414 | ISBN 9780367647957 (hardback) |
   ISBN 9780367647964 (paperback) | ISBN 9781003126324
   (ebook)
Subjects: LCSH: Banks and banking—Security measures—
   Case studies. | Confidential communications—Banking—
   Case studies. | Financial services industry—Security measures—
   Case studies.
Classification: LCC HG1616.S37 T73 2023 |
   DDC 332.1068—dc23/eng/20221027
LC record available at https://lccn.loc.gov/2022040414

ISBN: 978-0-367-64795-7 (hbk)
ISBN: 978-0-367-64796-4 (pbk)
ISBN: 978-1-003-12632-4 (ebk)

DOI: 10.4324/9781003126324

Typeset in Times New Roman
by Apex CoVantage, LLC

Contents

Illustrations

Figures

Tables

Preface

Modern financial markets have witnessed digital financial transformations owing to financial technology (FinTech) innovations. New market players such as FinTech startups providing services or products have been emerging in, for instance, the payment market thanks to their ability to reduce transaction costs by facilitating information flow. However, these startups often face barriers to market entry as the market and incumbent players have been so intertwined—defining the market's anticompetition tendencies. By removing the market-entry barriers, open banking (OB) policies can unleash the advantages of new market players while mitigating potential market failures. The regulatory approach urges or encourages incumbent financial institutions such as banks to open their data pools and application programming interfaces (APIs). To answer a core question probed in this book—"What policy implications can we draw from this comparison of OB policies between compulsory and voluntary approaches?"—we first examine the European and British "compulsory" approaches to OB before turning our focus toward the Taiwanese "voluntary" approach. Using the Taiwanese model as a case study, the book reveals implicit policy conundrums of mission conflicts and interest group influence while dialing in on organizational aspects of modern financial regulators from an institutional design perspective.

Against the market backdrop described here, the "compulsory" regulatory approach to OB, such as the second Payment Directive (PSD2) in the EU and its transposition in the UK has been introduced. In contrast, in Taiwan OB is promoted on a "voluntary" basis with the Financial Supervisory Commission's (FSC, the sole financial market watchdog in Taiwan) strong reliance on the ability of the banking industry to draft and implement OB self-regulation. Owing to the FSC's dependence on the banking industry, which would rather maintain the FSC's conservative posture in opening the FinTech door only to banks, FinTech businesses are increasingly directed by banks themselves. Similarly, under this model, the question remains as to whether incumbent banks are incentivized to open data pools to Fin-Tech startups, which are often regarded as potential bank competitors. Ulti-mately, such a voluntary approach appears less likely to attain the initial regulatory goals set under OB policies, that is, promoting financial inno-vation, competition, and inclusion. The pitfalls of Taiwan's voluntary OB approach could be explained theoretically from the public choice perspec-tive, illustrating how private interests influence and how banks might seek rents. As a result, we suspect that the pursuit of regulatory objectives in favor of public interests (i.e., achieving financial inclusion by way of pro-moting competition and innovation in financial markets) could be achieved as the OB regulatory regimes might in fact serve the interests of specific groups like incumbent banks.

As for the lessons learned from the Taiwanese case study, we provide some recommendations from the institutional design perspective. Namely, we suggest the implementation of an independent and professional regula-tor exclusively responsible for encouraging innovation and competition in a financial marketplace. As an independent entity, this regulator may not only be less vulnerable to undue influence but also, given its concentrated responsibilities, help avoid mission conflicts between prudential concerns and the promotion of competition and innovation in financial markets. To ease the problem of mission conflicts, this specialized regulator should be styled similar to the UK Competition and Markets Authority (CMA), which employs a more fundamental style of regulatory intervention to mitigate conflicts among FinTech innovation, competition, and consumer welfare (or financial inclusion) missions. By conferring these responsibilities upon this regulator, which is not fully subject to traditional financial regula-tors, the regulator can more effectively deliver the benefits of OB. As for candidates for such independent regulators, we propose, on the one hand, concentrating such a mission of promoting financial innovation and compe-tition on an independent regulator currently in Taiwan's executive branch, that is, the Fair Trade Commission (FTC, a government body similar to the UK's CMA). The new financial competition and innovation bureau under the FTC would specialize in promoting financial innovation and competi-tion at the same hierarchical level as the FSC. On the other hand, these FinTech-related tasks can be assigned to the "Ministry of Digital Affairs" (MDA) in Taiwan, which is being established. Given that people's demand for digital financial services is rising, this proposal would alleviate con-cerns that tasks related to digital finance have been largely ignored. Further-more, regarding the alternative structure we envision for the independent regulator, we discuss the form in which the regulatory authority would take, how "independent" such a regulator would need to be (e.g., to what degree it would be susceptible to oversight), and how to coordinate the inevitable overlap with the prudential or traditional sector regulator.

Based on the findings from our case study on Taiwan's OB regulation, an independent regulator, rather than a traditional sector regulator, could better resist influence by the banking industry, thereby realizing goals of advancing public interests such as fostering financial innovation, competition, and inclusion. That is, the comparison of OB policies between the "compulsory" British and EU initiatives and the "voluntary" Taiwanese model would, from a law and policy perspective, indicate that a compulsory approach might be preferable for implementing OB in Taiwan in particular. In general, this comparison would, from a regulatory-design point of view, illuminate that regulators aiming to promote financial innovation and competition in modern finance should be equipped with strong independency. Moreover, the institutional design perspective also provides insights when further designing this independent regulator.

The establishment of such an independent regulator should be subject to financial, procedural, and structural controls so as to ensure its accountability. However, the costs incurred by establishing the independent regulator and the associated regulations should not be ignored. Moreover, owing to the multifaceted legal issues in modern finance, it is critical that the traditional sector regulator and the regulator tasked to ensure financial innovation and competition collaborate and coordinate. In addition, we propose several regulatory arrangements for this independent financial regulator in light of our findings. First, we suggest that FinTech startups should participate in the rulemaking. Second, the process through which this independent regulator makes decisions should be transparent. Third, with respect to the structural control, this regulator should be composed of professionals less prone to influence by private interest groups such as industry associations; these professionals should also be involved in the process through which this independent regulator makes decisions.

Abbreviations

ABS	Association of Banks in Singapore
AISPs	account information services providers
APIs	application programming interfaces
ASPSPs	account servicing payment service providers
BaaP	banking-as-a-platform
BaaS	banking-as-a-service
BAROC	Bankers Association of the Republic of China (Taiwan)
CBC	Central Bank of the Republic of China (Taiwan)
CC	Competition Commission
CFPB	Consumer Financial Protection Bureau
CMA	Competition and Markets Authority
DMA	Digital Markets Act
DSA	Digital Services Act
EBA	European Banking Authority
ECF	equity crowdfunding
EU	European Union
FCA	Financial Conduct Authority
FCIB	financial competition and innovation bureau
FinTech	financial technology
FISC	Financial Information Service Co., Ltd.
FSA	Financial Service Authority
FSC	Financial Supervisory Commission
FSOC	Financial Stability Oversight Council
FTC	Fair Trade Commission
HKMA	Hong Kong Monetary Authority
JCIC	Joint Credit Information Center
MAS	Monetary Authority of Singapore
MDD	Ministry of Digital Development
NGO	non-governmental organization
NPO	non-profit organization

OAI	Open API Initiative
OAS	Open API Specification
OB	open banking
OBIE	Open Banking Implementation Entity
OFT	Office of Fair Trading
PaaS	platform-as-a-service
PCWs	price-comparison websites
PISPs	payment initiation services providers
PSD1	the first Payment Services Directive
PSD2	the second Payment Services Directive
PSRs 2017	the Payment Services Regulations 2017
PSU	payment service user
RTS	Regulatory Technical Standards
SEC	U.S. Securities and Exchange Commission
SMEs	small- and medium-sized enterprises
SRA	self-regulatory agency
SRO	self-regulatory organization
TPPs	third-party providers
TSPs	third-party service providers
UK	United Kingdom
US	United States
XS2A	access to account

1 Introduction

Compulsory versus Voluntary Approaches to Open Banking

Over recent years, modern financial markets have witnessed several transitions, which were unexpected before the 2008 global financial crisis.[1] Those transitions stem from, among other reasons, the rise of FinTech, which involves "digital innovations and technology-enabled business model innovations."[2] The benefits brought by FinTech across financial markets manifest as FinTech startups provide more alternatives to access to traditional financial services, thereby enhancing financial inclusion.[3] In addition, due to COVID-19's impact since late 2019, digital finance has drawn people's attention as it can help avoid human-to-human contact.[4] The pandemic also offered the opportunity for government regulators to reexamine their regulatory approaches to FinTech.[5] While the aforementioned benefits (or potential promises) are presented, some barriers to promoting FinTech remain; thus FinTech-oriented competition and innovation appear to be hindered to some extent. This book hence explores from a regulatory viewpoint the issues regarding the barriers to realizing FinTech's benefits by furthering FinTech competition and innovation.[6] In particular, in light of those barriers, what role should modern financial regulators play? This book, on the one hand, focuses on the structural design of modern financial regulators from an institutional design perspective.[7] On the other hand, we reveal the importance of the institutional settings regarding the elements critical to modern financial regulators in terms of regulating FinTech.[8] Specifically, this book focuses on OB, which has attracted enormous interest, as a means to realize the regulatory goal of enhancing and ensuring FinTech competition and innovation.[9] In other words, the idea of OB could be a solution to the aforementioned barriers to that goal, and regulators may play a crucial role in bringing about this solution.[10] Through the lens of the UK's and the EU's OB regulations, we will examine the OB regulatory policies in Taiwan as a case study to rethink the institutional design of financial regulators in the era of FinTech.

DOI: 10.4324/9781003126324-1

The nature of financial markets has been changed by the novel technologies and business models of new market players such as FinTech startups. In particular, FinTech startups have joined the financial markets where they could bring value and, thus, diversity by offering alternatives to conventional financial solutions. For instance, the payment markets, which have historically been intertwined with the traditional banking industry,[11] has been transformed by FinTech innovations and, therefore, in a sense decoupled from the legacy system thanks to the emergence of competing FinTech startups providing alternative financial services.[12] Accordingly, these new players may shape modern financial markets to the extent that they can be characterized as a digital system under which the goal of achieving financial inclusion could be ensured.[13] Put another way, the growth of digital finance allows a variety of new players to employ novel technologies and adopt innovative business models to provide access to financial services and hence promote financial inclusion.[14]

Nevertheless, although newly emerging FinTech startups are reshaping modern financial markets, some issues have arisen. Specifically, even though new entrants have flourished—providing the aforementioned socially beneficial services, entry barriers, for example, in payment markets where incumbent banks have predominantly controlled the customer data pools, remain in the financial sector.[15] Thus, FinTech startups might be hindered in their efforts to enter the market.[16] These issues are heightened in the FinTech era given that information plays a crucial role in digital finance, where the amount of data amassed by individual players determines their competitive strength.[17] Consequently, while FinTech startups are capable of benefiting the market by, for instance, facilitating payment transactions by integrating financial data, the difficulty in accessing the data forecloses the realization of these benefits.[18] Regulatory intervention, as provided by the EU's PSD2 and the UK's OB initiative, offers solutions[19] as it takes into consideration the importance of information in the era of digital finance by mandating the openness of customers' data held by incumbent banks. Furthermore, regulatory intervention "aim[s] at promoting competition by empowering customers to exploit their own data,"[20] which demonstrates just as the regulations shape the modern financial markets, so too does information.[21]

By contrast, some frictions are found in the design and/or implementation of FinTech regulation aimed to promote financial innovation and competition in Taiwan,[22] possibly resulting in the regulatory failures that have been historically shown.[23] Implicit in these frictions and failures are that, among others, the regulatory regimes might serve the interests of specific groups,[24] and these minority but concentrated interests may prevail over those of the public.[25] These phenomena are critical as the contemporary Taiwanese financial markets are controlled by the corresponding regulations.[26] Since the phenomena of rent-seeking could be observed in the Taiwanese context, it is doubtful that we could attain the regulatory objectives (achieving financial inclusion and promoting competition and innovation in the financial markets) in favor of such public interests.[27]

We study the European and British regulatory strategies in promoting OB from a more conceptual perspective; then, we examine the Taiwanese OB policies as a case study. We thereby reveal the implicit policy conundrum mentioned here, rethinking the institutional design of financial regulators in the era of FinTech. Specifically, this book supports a regulatory design view that OB policies might help establish an institutional infrastructure for a financial marketplace by opening data pools, supporting the development of FinTech ecosystems.[28] This discussion is distinguished from the existing literature as we analyze the EU's and the UK's experiences in OB by emphasizing their "compulsory" policies and focusing on the aspect of the institutional design of financial regulators. Therefore, this book fills a gap as this theoretical perspective seems to be comparatively lacking in the current OB literature. Furthermore, this book contributes to the discussion of how a regulatory-design approach addresses the limitations of traditional sector regulators in promoting financial innovation and competition. Specifically, recrafting the institutional arrangements thereof, that is, conferring authority of promoting financial competition and innovation upon a more motivated regulator, will be our core idea.[29]

This book is divided into five chapters. Chapter 2 emphasizes theoretical grounds on which we will explain the OB regulations in response to the regulatory challenges brought by FinTech. This chapter also explores the importance of information in the era of FinTech and the associated regulatory issues. Chapter 3 then discusses OB regulations in the UK and the EU, elaborating on how such regulatory regimes serve as the infrastructure that helps foster financial innovation and competition via,[30] for instance, an emphasis on the role of regulators. Next, Chapter 4 turns the focus on the OB regulations in Taiwan from a comparative view. This chapter, given the lessons of the EU's and the UK's experiences, examines what obstacles would exist when boosting financial innovation and competition in the age of FinTech in Taiwan. Specifically, concerns remain that certain public interests (i.e., promoting financial innovation and competition) may be dwarfed since Taiwan's current OB policies would result in regulatory pitfalls. On a practical level, the major obstacle to promoting financial innovation and competition in Taiwan might be derived from the incumbent banking industry's resistance. On a theoretical level, the OB regulatory policies in Taiwan illustrate how private interests might prevail in the public realm as banks could seek rents. A single traditional financial regulator like the Financial Supervisory Commission (FSC) in Taiwan may be easily influenced by regulated banks, and, as a result, financial competition and innovation would rank low on their priority list.[31]

After summarizing the findings from the previous chapters, Chapter 5 concludes the book, using an institutional design perspective to propose that an independent regulator—not subject to the traditional sector regulator like the FSC in Taiwan—will be needed. Based on the lessons learned from the Taiwanese case study and the concomitant comparative analysis, we offer suggestions regarding how to craft this regulator's structure. For instance, we recommend potential candidates for this regulator in Taiwan. Moreover, we also elaborate on possible organizational arrangements for this regulator.

Notes

1 *See* Douglas W. Arner, Jànos Barberis, & Ross P. Buckley, *FinTech, RegTech, and the Reconceptualization of Financial Regulation*, 37 Nw. J. Int'l L. & Bus. 371, 373 (2017).

2 Thomas Philippon, *On Fintech and Financial Inclusion* 2 (NBER Working Paper No. 26330, 2019), www.nber.org/papers/w26330. The idea of the employment of new technologies to deliver financial solutions including services and products is as known as "FinTech." Arner et al., *supra* note 1, at 373.

3 The G20 Principles advocate providing "an enabling and proportionate legal and regulatory framework for digital financial inclusion." GPFI, *G20 High-Level Principles for Digital Financial Inclusion* 1 (2016). This could be because financial inclusion can accelerate economic growth. Purva Khera, Stephanie Ng, Sumiko Ogawa, & Ratna Sahay, *Is Digital Financial Inclusion Unlocking Growth?* 14 (IMF Working Paper, June 2021), https://ssrn.com/abstract=4026364.

4 *See* Douglas W. Arner, Jànos Nathan Barberis, Julia Walker, Ross P. Buckley, Andrew M. Dahdal, & Dirk A. Zetzsche, *Digital Finance & COVID-19 Crisis* 2 (University of Hong Kong Faculty of Law Research Paper No. 2020/017, UNSW Law Research), https://ssrn.com/abstract=3558889. Indeed, the design of regulation for digital areas has been an attractive contemporary issue. *See* Andrew Murray, *Rethinking Regulation for the Digital Environment*, 41 LSE L. Pol'y Briefing Series 1, 2 (2019).

5 Julie Andersen Hill, *COVID-19 and FinTech* 5 (University of Alabama Legal Studies Research Paper No. 3777562, 2021), https://ssrn.com/abstract=3777562.

6 *See* Ross P. Buckley, Douglas W. Arner, & Dirk A. Zetzsche, *Sustainability, FinTech and Financial Inclusion* 7 (European Banking Institute Working Paper Series 2019/41; UNSW Law Research Paper No. 19–63; University of Hong Kong Faculty of Law Research Paper No. 2019/038, May 22, 2019), https://ssrn.com/abstract=3387359.

7 From a higher perspective, "institutional design" is associated with the arrangement, form, and function of social institutions, which vary on a discipline-by-discipline basis. *See* Robert E. Goodin, *Institutions and Their Design, in* The Theory of Institutional Design 1, 1 (Robert E. Goodin ed., Cambridge University Press, 1996) (http://doi.org/10.1017/CBO9780511558320.002). As such, from

the viewpoint of political science, which is one of the disciplines of institutional design theory, the structural or organizational design of government agencies is an important issue. *See id.* at 11–12. Following this path, this book analyzes the structural design of financial regulators in the context of FinTech. Similarly, commentators suggested that the role of regulators in establishing FinTech regulations should be re-examined by considering social circumstances. *See, for example*, David C. Donald, *Hong Kong's Fintech Automation: Economic Benefits and Social Risks* 19–20 (The Chinese University of Hong Kong Faculty of Law Research Paper No. 2020–05), https://ssrn.com/abstract=3544072.

8 It could be observed in literature that the institutional setup is one of the important elements of improving modern regulation. For instance, in the school of responsive regulation, the aspect of institutions has been well studied. *See* Julia Black & Robert Baldwin, *Really Responsive Risk-Based Regulation*, 32 Law & Pol'y 181, 186, 194 (2010); Ian Ayres & John Braithwaite, *Responsive Regulation: Transcending the Deregulation Debate* 17–18, 97 (Oxford University Press, 1992) (https://doi.org/10.1093/oxfordhb/9780199646135.013.40). In the arena of designing FinTech regulation, this aspect has been emphasized as well. *See, for example*, Chang-Hsien Tsai, *To Regulate or Not to Regulate? A Comparison of Government Responses to Peer-to-Peer Lending among the United States, China, and Taiwan*, 87 U. Cin. L. Rev. 1077, 1109 (2019).

9 The term "open banking" refers conceptually to the sharing of data such as customers' data by the use of open application programming interfaces ("APIs") to enable third parties to access and use such data in a safe and resilient way. EBA Working Group on Electronic Alternative Payments, *Understanding the Business Relevance of Open APIs and Open Banking for Banks: Information Paper* 15 (2016). APIs are interfaces where different software applications could communicate with each other when one would call upon the functionality of another. However, APIs could be accessed either within or beyond the boundaries of an organization. If an API could be accessed by third parties, it is a public interface to access data based on an open standard. This is the so-called "open APIs." *Id.* at 7; Open Banking Working Group, *The Open Banking Standard: Unlocking the Potential of Open banking to Improve Competition, Efficiency and Stimulate Innovation* 4 (2016).

10 *See The Dash from Cash: Rich Countries Must Start Planning for a Cashless Future*, The Economist, Aug. 3 2019, at 9–10; Giuseppe Colangelo & Oscar Borgogno, *Data, Innovation and Transatlantic Competition in Finance: The Case of the Access to Account Rule* 7, 29 (EU L. Working Papers No. 35, 2018), https://www-cdn.law.stanford.edu/wp-content/uploads/2018/09/colangelo_borgogno_eulawwp35.pdf.

11 Dan Awrey & Kristin van Zwieten, *The Shadow Payment System*, 43 J. Corp. L. 775, 776, 784 (2018).

12 *See id.* at 777–78.

13 *See* Ross P. Buckley & Louise Malady, *The New Regulatory Frontier: Building Consumer Demand for Digital Financial Services – Part I*, 131 Banking L. J. 834, 834–35 (2014).

14 *See id.* at 835. This phenomenon is interpreted by using the term "digital financial services" (or "DFS") to stress the role played by some new financial instruments or institutions in ensuring financial inclusion. *Id.* at 834. Meanwhile, we use the term "digital finance" to broadly refer to the transformation of financial markets with the entry of FinTech startups, benefiting consumers by combining

finance and technological innovation. Arner et al., *supra* note 1, at 381. In addition to FinTech startups, large technology companies (namely "BigTechs") are getting involved in modern financial markets as well. BigTech firms have recently been involved in financial industry by incorporating financial services to their value-chains, turning "TechFins." Typical examples in China are Alibaba and Tencent as they dominate the payment markets. *See* Dirk A. Zetzsche, Ross P. Buckley, Douglas W. Arner, & Janos N. Barberis, *From Fintech to Techfin: The Regulatory Challenges of Data-Driven Finance*, 14 N.Y.U. J. L. & Bus. 393, 405, 407, 410 (2018); Jon Frost, Leonardo Gambacorta, Yi Huang, Hyun Song Shin, & Pablo Zbinden, *BigTech and the Changing Structure of Financial Intermediation* 2–3 (BIS Working Papers No. 779, Apr. 2019), www.bis.org/publ/work779.pdf.

15 *See* Colangelo & Borgogno, *supra* note 10, at 10, 29–30. As discussed in the note 14, in addition to the threats posed by incumbent banks, the introduction of BigTechs to financial markets poses network effects, and they are therefore able to extract value and to discriminate against other players including incumbent financial institutions. *See* Miguel de la Mano & Jorge Padilla, *Big Tech Banking*, 14 J. Competition L. & Econ. 494, 507 (2019); Dirk A. Zetzsche, Douglas W. Arner, Ross P. Buckley, & Rolf H. Weber, *The Future of Data-Driven Finance and RegTech: Lessons from EU Big Bang II* 25 (EBI Working Paper Series No. 35; UNSW L. Research Series No. 19–22, 2019), https://ssrn.com/abstract=3359399. The concerns such as consumer protection, stemming from BigTech's involvement in financial services, thereby called for a proposal in the United States to exclude them from financial markets. Pete Schroeder & Ismail Shakil, *U.S. Proposes Barring Big Tech Companies from Offering Financial Services, Digital Currencies*, Reuters (July 15, 2019), www.reuters.com/article/us-usa-cryptocurrency-bill/u-s-proposes-barring-big-tech-companies-from-offering-financial-services-digital-currencies-idUSKCN1U90NL.

16 Colangelo & Borgogno, *supra* note 10, at 10.

17 Zetzsche et al., *supra* note 15, at 25. As for how BigTechs exploit the large amount of customers' transactional data they gather, *see* René M. Stulz, *FinTech, BigTech, and Future of Banks* 19–21 (Fisher College of Bus. Working Paper Series No. 2019–03–020, Sep. 2019), https://ssrn.com/abstract=3455297.

18 *See* Cristina Poncibó & Oscar Borgogno, *Law and Autonomous Systems Series: The Day After Tomorrow of Banking – On FinTech, Data Control and Consumer Empowerment*, Oxford Bus. L. Blog (Apr. 5, 2018), www.law.ox.ac.uk/business-law-blog/blog/2018/04/law-and-autonomous-systems-series-day-after-tomorrow-banking-fintech.

19 Directive 2015/2366, Amending Directives 2002/65/EC, 2009/110/EC and 2013/36/EU and Regulation (EU) No 1093/2010, and Repealing Directive 2007/64/EC, 2015 O.J. (L 337) 35 [hereinafter Directive 2015/2366]. PSD2 had to be implemented in the UK since the UK had not left the European Union yet when PSD2 was under drafting and then came into force. *PS17/19: Implementation of the revised Payment Services Directive (PSD2)*, Financial Conduct Authority (Sep. 20, 2017), www.fca.org.uk/publications/policy-statements/ps17-19-implementation-revised-payment-services-directive (describing that "[t]he revised Payment Services Directive (PSD2) is required to be implemented in the UK by 13 January 2018."). As we will discuss, both PSD2 and UK's Open Banking aim to help the newly emerging third-party providers in the payment markets obtain information, and they are called "TPPs" (third-party

providers). *See* Chapter 3, Section 1.2. The counterpart of TPPs in the context of Taiwan's OB is called "TSPs" (third-party service providers). However, as we will explain in more detail, TSPs and TPPs are similar because of the similar entities they refer to literally while the scope of the former seems broader. *See* Chapter 4, Section 2.1.3 and Section 2.1.7. This book, nevertheless, uses different terms according to respective jurisdictions whose policies are discussed.

20 Poncibó & Borgogno, *supra* note 18. Therefore, this book will at first emphasize the importance of information in the digital finance and the related legal issues. *See* Chapter 2. Then, this book moves to discuss the regulatory responses such as PSD2 and UK's Open Banking as these regulatory initiatives reflected on the importance of information from the angle of intuitional design. *See* Chapter 3.

21 *See, for example*, David C. Donald, *Information, and the Regulation of Inefficient Markets*, *in* The Political Economy of Financial Regulation 38, 38, 54–57 (Emilios Avgouleas & David C. Donald eds., Cambridge University Press, 2019) (https://doi.org/10.1017/9781108612821.003); Zetzsche et al., *supra* note 15, at 10. Thus, "information" shapes the modern financial markets and regulations applied to it since how information is distributed and whether prices appropriately reflect it determine when regulation is necessary. *See* Donald, *supra* note 21, at 38. Similarly, "data," which could be viewed as a practical type of information, shapes the modern financial markets because new players emerge with their enhanced skills to use data; hence modern regulations focus on, for instance, the general protection of data and information sharing (or openness of data). Zetzsche et al., *supra* note 15, at 48–50. This book is formulated in accordance with the aforementioned ideas, especially from the angle of competition policy demonstrated in PSD2 and UK's Open Banking. *See id.* at 26 (arguing that there is "the policy demand to treat data as a product, since *information and data* although different from traditional goods and services, pose problems familiar to competition / antitrust law, such as monopolistic behavior and collusion.") (emphasis added). In this book, however, the term "information" will be used mainly, but the term "data" will also be used especially when referring to a more practical, specific, and narrow meaning.

22 As discussed in more detail in Chapter 4, Section 3.1, Article 1 of the FinTech Sandbox Act, which was enacted on January 31, 2018, was aimed to promote innovation in financial services or products, financial inclusion, and FinTech development as its main regulatory objectives. Jin Rong Ke Ji Fa Zhan Yu Chuang Xin Shi Yan Tiao Li (金融科技發展與創新實驗條例) [Financial Technology Development and Innovative Experimentation Act] (hereinafter the "FinTech Sandbox Act"), art. 1. *See also* Ross P. Buckley, Douglas Arner, Robin Veidt, & Dirk Zetzsche, *Building FinTech Ecosystems: Regulatory Sandboxes, Innovation Hubs and Beyond* 21 (UNSW Research Paper No. 19–72, 2019), https://ssrn.com/abstract=3455872 (highlighting that "[a] sandbox and/or an innovation hub are designed to promote innovation and competition.").

23 *See* Tsai, *supra* note 8, at 1118–19.

24 *See* George J. Stigler, *The Theory of Economic Regulation*, 2 Bell J. Econ. & Manage. Sci. 3, 3–4 (1971).

25 Therefore, efficiency would not be achieved in that "private interest groups thwart the democratic process" and that "concentrated, minority economic interests prevail over the more widespread, majority economic interests." Anthony I. Ogus, *Regulation: Legal Form and Economic Theory* 24–25, 71–73 (Hart Publishing, 2004) (http://dx.doi.org/10.5040/9781472559647).

26 *See* Chapter 4, Section 1. Law in a sense determines rules of games in financial markets, which can thus be described to be constructed by the legal system. *See, for example*, Katharina Pistor, *A Legal Theory of Finance*, 41 J. Comp. Econ. 315, 315, 317–18, 321–25 (2013); Simon Deakin, *The Legal Theory of Finance: Implications for the Methodology and Empirical Research*, 41 J. Comp. Econ. 338, 338, 340 (2013); Dan Awrey, *Law and Finance in the Chinese Shadow Banking System*, 48 Cornell Int'l L. J. 1, 10 (2015).

27 *See* Chapter 4, Section 3; Ogus, *supra* note 25, at 71 (explaining private interest theories of regulation by illustrating regulatory "measures which ostensibly protect more generalized interests, such as consumers or the environment, but which serve to generate profits for the industries or firms (or some of them) which are regulated."). For further explanations, *see also id.* at 56, 59, 72–73; John Armour, Dan Awrey, Paul Davies, Luca Enriques, Jeffrey N. Gordon, Colin Mayer, & Jennifer Payne, *Principles of Financial Regulation* 560–62 (Oxford University Press, 2016) (http://doi.org/10.1093/acprof:oso/9780198786474.003.0017) (examining different channels of regulatory capture as one of the regulatory failures).

28 *See* Mark Fenwick & Erik P. M. Vermeulen, *Banking and Regulatory Responses to FinTech Revisited: Building the Sustainable Financial Service 'Ecosystems' of Tomorrow* 32 (LEX Research Topics in Corp. L. & Econ. Working Paper No. 2019–4, 2019), https://ssrn.com/abstract=3446273. *See also* Ross P. Buckley et al., *The Dark Side of Digital Financial Transformation: The New Risks of FinTech and the Rise of TechRisk* 2–3 (EBI Working Paper 2019/54; UNSW L. Research Series No. 19–89, 2019), https://ssrn.com/abstract=3478640 (discussing four major axes of the process of digital financial transformation).

29 A regulatory-design approach could address the limitations of sector regulators such as their unwillingness to protect competition and innovation in the regulated financial markets. Samuel N. Weinstein, *Financial Regulation in the (Receding) Shadow of Antitrust*, 91 Temp. L. Rev. 447, 495, 512 (2019). A structural regulatory approach that prohibits anti-competitive conduct ex ante was argued to be more favorable. *Id.* at 495, 507–8, 512. This book is initially inspired by this study as it provides regulatory-design solutions to the limitations of sector regulators in being competent guardians of competition. However, we will propose a way to address this issue by re-designing the institutional design of regulators in the financial sector after drawing an inclusive theory from our comparison among the EU, UK, and Taiwan experiences.

30 *See* Douglas W. Arner, Ross P. Buckley, & Dirk A. Zetzsche, *Fintech for Financial Inclusion: A Framework for Digital Financial Transformation* 7 (2018), www.afi-global.org/sites/default/files/publications/2018-09/AFI_FinTech_Special%20Report_AW_digital.pdf (noting that "[s]upportive infrastructure and an enabling policy and regulatory environment" are of vital importance to encourage financial inclusion in the digital financial ecosystem). For example, a well-designed regulatory strategy to set up sandboxes and/or innovation hubs, which would enable a broader scope of industry to assess their innovative services or products, can support the FinTech ecosystem and promote financial competition and innovation. *See* Buckley et al., *supra* note 22, at 5, 21, 26–27.

31 *See* Weinstein, *supra* note 29, at 452.

2 A New Era of Financial Innovation: Information as an Important Factor in Shaping the Modern Financial Market

This chapter examines the new FinTech era by exploring the key factors (e.g., information) for deciding whether the regulatory system should respond to it; and, if so, how such responses should be formulated. Financial transformations that shape this new era do not necessarily justify regulatory intervention.[1] Therefore, instead of merely examining justifications for new regulations, this chapter investigates the role of information in shaping both the modern digital finance and the associated regulations to be imposed. In addition, this chapter lays the groundwork for discussing OB promotion (i.e., the openness of data) via regulations.[2]

This chapter is divided into three sections. Section 1 illustrates what underpins the modern digital finance from a theoretical perspective. This section considers the emergence of new players, particularly FinTech start-ups who provide financial services—looking specifically at how these new players facilitate information flow, reduce transaction costs, and reshape the financial sectors, which have been long-intertwined with incumbent banks. Section 2 then analyzes the regulatory issues in relation to the rise of these new players by studying, for example, rationales for regulatory intervention. Section 3 summarizes the investigation, findings, and suggestions.

1. Setting the Scene—Modern Digital Finance and the Development of Platform-Based Business Models

As a general phenomenon, modern markets have manifested themselves as the permeation and diffusion of platform-based business models because of their employment of novel technologies.[3] As the ecosystems serving to facilitate the interactions or transactions between the consumers on the demand side and the merchants on the supply side,[4] platforms are regarded as an important component in transactions by connecting suppliers and users.[5] As we will further explain, the success of this platform-based business model is due, theoretically, to new players' ability to facilitate

DOI: 10.4324/9781003126324-2

transactions and reduce the associated transaction costs.[6] Similarly in the context of OB, it appears that the openness of APIs, as the interfaces that connect transactional participants by bringing crucial resources together, is enhanced by OB.[7]

Given that modern financial markets are characterized by platform-based business models, which are exemplified by the concept of OB, this section further discusses the nature of the modern digital finance and that of OB from a more conceptual viewpoint. That is, this section considers how and to what extent modern digital finance and/or the OB ecosystem reflects reduced transaction costs by technological enablers therein such as open APIs.[8] Put another way, an advantage of the platform-based business model is the potential to lower transaction costs.[9] Transaction cost reductions are possible because platforms improve the coordination between different parties in the market and increase the likelihood of being matched or connected.[10] Commentators contend that these benefits could also be realized in the case of OB through the implementation of open APIs.[11]

The discussion here encompasses two critical elements—the players who realize platform-based business models and the information facilitated by these players. The role of new market participants is pivotal. In the case of OB, these FinTech startups operate as platforms facilitating information, such as transaction data, that is shared by incumbent banks through open APIs as required in European and British OB reforms.[12] Accordingly, the concept of Banking-as-a-Service (BaaS) would be realized through OB owing to the sharing of information through open APIs.[13] Along this line, it could be observed that enhancing access to information is critical to the formation of the modern digital finance where platform-based business models are prevalent,[14] thereby characterizing the FinTech era as a "modern form of money" therein.[15]

2.　Emergence of New Market Participants and Related Regulatory Issues

2.1　*Emergence of the New Market Participants Involved in the Platform-Based Business Models*

After setting the scene above from a higher-level perspective, this section analyzes participation of new market players based on the platform-based businesses models and associated regulatory issues. In the context of FinTech, "platformization" has been regarded as a feature of the FinTech era as players exist as platforms that provide services digitally.[16] Regulators' efforts amid this rise of the platform-based business model are not limited to OB regulations. For instance, the recent regulatory developments are the

EU Digital Services Act (DSA) and Digital Markets Act (DMA) that were proposed in 2020 to include online intermediaries and platforms into the regulatory scope.[17] This writing, however, focuses only on the OB regulations within those recent regulatory developments.

OB mirrors the rise of platform-based business models that would bring changes to traditional financial markets.[18] This platform-based model also contains characteristics of disruptive innovation that "connote of genuine '*change*' with *substitutive potential* that ultimately produces *structural impact*."[19] Moreover, based on this business model, newly emerging service providers are important alternatives to traditional banking thanks to their ability to facilitate different functions "at the so-called front-end and end-to-end levels" with the application of technology.[20] Therefore, these new market participants—who introduce novelty—may challenge incumbents or even replace them.[21]

As a matter of fact, the new market participants, who are challenging existing incumbents, include not merely smaller-sized firms such as FinTech startups but also larger-sized technology companies, namely BigTechs or TechFins like Tencent and Alibaba (Ant Financial).[22] These companies provide financial services or products and compete with incumbent financial institutions by leveraging their various advantages such as the informational advantage,[23] the technological advantage,[24] and the reputational advantage.[25] The informational advantage, in particular, boosts modern digital finance as it grants nonbank new market players better access to information, allowing them to compete with incumbent financial institutions such as traditional banks.[26]

2.2 Regulatory Issues—The Development of Open Banking Policies to Mitigate Market Failures

2.2.1 Overview

According to commentators, the emergence of new market players has the potential to prompt the aforementioned disruptive consequences of innovation, that is, genuine "change," "substitutive potential," and "structural impact." Given that such innovation may inform regulatory thinking,[27] this section examines the likely regulatory issues and associated regulatory responses across jurisdictions that subsequently transpire with the rise of new market players.[28]

Technological development has promoted innovation and enabled various new players to enter financial markets.[29] Due to the likelihood of market failures arising from this phenomenon an array of potential regulatory issues arise.[30] The role of governments in promoting innovation while simultaneously mitigating market failures should not be ignored.[31] This section focuses on the regulatory issues that are relatively foundational, while Section 2.3 will point out that—in the context of modern digital finance—a different and creative regulatory intervention should be adopted to avoid hampering innovation.[32] As discussed earlier, modern digital finance is centered around information.[33] As such, when participatory entities involved in the payment markets are diversified, two main issues merit attention—information asymmetry and anticompetition.[34] These two issues establish the grounds for enacting OB regulations such as PSD2 as they exemplify the market failures that OB regulations aim to mitigate.[35] We delve into those two issues next in the context of OB.

2.2.2 Information Asymmetry in Information-Driven Finance

First, issues of information are particularly important in modern financial markets where the information control influences how the markets function.[36] An inherent information asymmetry exists between consumers and providers of products or services. In theory, the information asymmetry, which would generate an adverse selection problem, is particularly relevant to the objective that regulators seek to pursue—ensuring the protection of consumers and investors.[37] Regulatory intervention is therefore justified in part as these consumers or investors may be exploited because of the principal-agent problem and/or the lack of adequate or accurate information about their decisions. In other words, consumers or investors may be unable to assess, for instance, the quality of financial contracts when purchasing, due to either the aforementioned issues or consumers' under-investment in information.[38]

However, in the context of modern financial markets in particular, a study argued that the aforementioned conundrum where consumers and investors encounter information asymmetry may be eased by the emergence of FinTech startups, which increase consumers' ability to assess and compare financial services and products with the aid of technology.[39] OB regulations, such as PSD2, contribute critically to these changes as they mitigate such information asymmetry by ensuring that FinTech startups can gain the information needed to provide such services.[40] Furthermore, these regulations enable those consumers and investors to exploit their own data, leading to the phenomenon that both modern financial markets and the corresponding regulation hinge on the role of information.[41]

2.2.3 Anticompetition Tendencies in the Payment Sector

The anticompetitive tendency is the other regulatory issue that OB reforms aim to tackle.[42] This issue arises in financial markets where various payment alternatives are offered by different services providers.[43] Generally speaking, a market imperfection leading to market failures would impair competition.[44] Financial regulation literature has stressed the need to reinforce competition; in fact, one of the policy tools for protecting consumers supported by such literature is competition enhancement.[45] As such, several conditions, such as the presence of a large number of small producers and the free entry of new entrants, should be fulfilled in order to achieve a competitive market. These conditions help allocate resources in an appropriate way to places in which resources would generate the greatest benefit.[46]

Nevertheless, the anticompetitive tendency in the payment sector is apparent in, for instance, the network effects stemming from the rise of BigTechs and the concentration (or even the dominance) by incumbent banks. We focus our discussion on the role of the latter.[47] The incumbent banks' dominance is associated with the limited competition that exists historically in the markets.[48] Scholars have argued that, in the last two decades, the banking sector has become highly concentrated.[49] Studies have shown that when large banks have greater influence—inducing banking concentration—there is resulting limitation to financial access and reduction in competition. Accordingly, such impacts may systemically harm financial markets.[50] Yet, due to the market power of these large banks, impaired competition may merely be deemed one source of social cost.[51] That is, their market power exists at the expense of smaller players such as FinTech startups that face entry barriers, for example, the inability to obtain access to information or data as it has been traditionally controlled by incumbent large banks.[52]

Above all, the aforementioned regulatory issues regarding information asymmetry and anticompetition tendency also reflect the historical trade-offs between the existing and new objectives that regulators intend to attain simultaneously. This idea of mission conflict denotes the regulatory dilemma between traditional goals, such as ensuring financial stability or consumer protection, and new ones, such as promoting financial competition, innovation, and inclusion.[53] When regulators aim to address such dilemmas, they may fail to address each goal simultaneously due to, for example, the potential failure in the institutional design of financial regulators.[54]

2.3 Frictions in Modern Digital Finance and the Role of Regulators—Factoring in Information, Innovation, and Regulation

We explained earlier that, in the context of OB, information plays a crucial role in modern digital finance[55] and the ramifications of OB regulations relate to the payment sector where a diversity of participants emerges.[56] We then sketched a broad overview of digital transformations in modern finance. Before turning to our examination of the regulatory responses in practice,[57] we take a peek into the frictions implicit in modern digital finance and discuss what role regulators can play to address them.

A friction lies between the control of information and the promotion of innovation. While a handful of financial institutions control access to information, emerging players such as FinTech startups would face barriers to access to, for example, the payment services market because they lack access to the information critical to their ability to provide services.[58] Consequently, competition is repressed, and innovation is stifled as the FinTech startups are thereby prevented from implementing their innovative business models.[59] Both impacts contribute to a decline in consumer welfare.[60] In other words, while FinTech-driven innovation could facilitate financial markets by creating more opportunities for consumers to access finance, the lack of information may hamper this possibility. In a sense, an introduction of a proper regulatory intervention such as the EU's PSD2 or the UK's OB initiative might be the cure.[61] Nonetheless, a friction could also be found between regulation and innovation.[62] For example, a burdensome, uncertain, or improperly designed regulation may actually impede innovation.[63] The EU has long focused on the problem of balancing the need for regulation and the promotion of innovation.[64] "Better regulation" emphasizes not only a greater possibility the regulatory goals could be achieved (and at lower costs) but also the outcome that competition and innovation could be fostered by regulation.[65] As such, the issue of how to regulate in the era of FinTech in particular (or in the era of innovation in general) is pivotal. Specifically, it is contended that "innovation and regulation are in a reflexive relationship with one another";[66] for instance, "particularly fast-moving innovations can generate information and data problems for regulators."[67] Therefore, as we presented, information issues play an important role in the operation of modern finance with FinTech innovations.[68]

In addition to designing regulation in a manner that fosters competition and innovation, another possible solution involves designing regulators themselves.[69] Hence, we argue that in order to promote financial competition and innovation—and thus to benefit digital financial inclusion, there should be, among other things, an appropriate organizational design for professional regulators to achieve these modern regulatory goals in chorus.[70] Taking OB reforms as an example, we will further examine, in Chapters 3 and 4, what an appropriate institutional design of financial regulators looks like so as to promote financial innovation and competition.

3. Conclusion

From a theoretical perspective, this chapter established the foundations for regulatory responses in modern digital finance in the context of OB. We discussed the potential concern that information asymmetry and anticompetition could haunt digital financial transformations. New market players complement or even substitute for incumbent players in the payment sector given their ability to facilitate informational flow, thereby reducing transaction costs. However, due to other existing hurdles, it is doubtful that these benefits could be reaped. One such hurdle is the anticompetition tendency, which prohibits those benefits from being unleashed as new players cannot obtain the information critical to their provision of services in the payment sector. At a practical level, we now embark on the examination of the regulatory responses to the aforementioned conundrum, such as OB reforms in the UK and the EU. We will consider their experiences to determine how best to carry out the institutional design of financial regulators in favor of the promotion of financial innovation and competition.

Notes

1 On the one hand, financial transformation may negatively influence consumer protection because BigTechs or TechFins as new players are not subject to existing regulations; in this case, regulation may be necessary. Dirk A. Zetzsche, Ross P. Buckley, Douglas W. Arner, & Janos N. Barberis, *From Fintech to Techfin: The Regulatory Challenges of Data-Driven Finance*, 14 N.Y.U. J. L. & Bus. 393, 430–31 (2018). On the other hand, compared to traditional banks, which are heavily regulated, FinTech firms are less regulated, and less regulation might spur innovation. *See* René M. Stulz, *FinTech, BigTech, and Future of Banks* 12–14 (Fisher College of Bus. Working Paper Series No. 2019–03–020, Sep. 2019), https://ssrn.com/abstract=3455297.

2 The openness of data that would establish an open ecosystem could support digital transformations in financial markets. *See* Mark Fenwick & Erik P. M. Vermeulen, *Banking and Regulatory Responses to FinTech Revisited: Building the Sustainable Financial Service 'Ecosystems' of Tomorrow* 5, 21, 27–28, 32 (LEX Research Topics in Corp. L. & Econ. Working Paper No. 2019-4, 2019), https://ssrn.com/abstract=3446273.

3 *See* Markos Zachariadis & Pinar Ozcan, *The API Economy and Digital Transformation in Financial Services: The Case of Open Banking* 6–7 (SWIFT Inst. Working Paper No. 2016–001, June 15, 2017), https://ssrn.com/abstract=2975199; Annabelle Gawer & Rebecca Henderson, *Platform Owner Entry and Innovation in Complementary Markets: Evidence from Intel*, 16 J. Econ. & Mgmt. Strategy 1, 1–2 (2007); Elisabeth Noble, *Digital Platform: A New Source of Financial System Interconnectedness*, Oxford Business Law Blog (Sep. 27, 2021), www.law.ox.ac.uk/business-law-blog/blog/2021/09/digital-platforms-new-source-financial-system-interconnectedness-0.

4 *See* Zachariadis & Ozcon, *supra* note 3, at 6; Jean-Charles Rochet & Jean Tirole, *Two-Sided Markets: A Progress Report*, 37 RAND J. Econ. 645, 645 (2006); Jean-Charles Rochet & Jean Tirole, *Platform Competition in Two-Sided Markets*, 1 J. Eur. Econ. Ass'n. 990, 990–91, 995 (2003). We, however, do not intend to comprehensively define and analyze platforms to give any normative implications. Regarding different definitions of platforms, *see, for example*, Gawer & Henderson, *supra* note 3, at 4 (defining a "platform" as "one component or subsystem of an evolving technological system, when it is strongly functionally interdependent with most of the other components of this system, and when end-user demand is for the overall system, so that there is no demand for components when they are isolated from the overall system.").

5 *See* Zachariadis & Ozcon, *supra* note 3, at 7.

6 *See* Section 2.1.

7 *See* Zachariadis & Ozcon, *supra* note 3, at 7–8.

8 *See id.*; EBA Open Banking Working Group, *Open Banking: Advancing Customer-centricity – Analysis and Overview* 20–21 (Mar. 2017).

9 *See* Michael Munger, *Coase and the "Sharing Economy," in* Forever Contemporary: The Economics of Ronald Coase 187, 190 (Cento Veljanovski ed., Institute of Economic Affairs, 2015) (arguing that the current transaction costs revolution features "much more intensive use of existing goods and skills of service providers," which has been called the "sharing economy" by many). In regard to the Coase theorem, *see* R. H. Coase, *The Problem of Social Cost*, 3 J. L. & Econ. 1, 8 (1960); R. H. Coase, *The Nature of the Firm*, 4 Economica 386, 390 (1937). There is a great deal of relevant literature discussing and explaining the Coase theorem. For example, it is argued that the misallocation of resources could be overcome in the market by bargains if the assumptions of rationality and zero transaction costs hold; thus, efficiency could be achieved. Guido Calabresi, *Transaction Costs, Resource Allocation, and Liability Rules: A Comment*, 11 J. L. & Econ. 67, 68 (1968). *See also* A. Mitchell Polinsky, *Economic Analysis as a Potentially Defective Product: A Buyer's Guide to Posner's "Economic Analysis of Law,"* 87 Harv. L. Rev. 1655, 1665 (1974) (summarizing Richard Posner's methodological theme: "If transaction costs are zero the structure of the law does not matter because efficiency will result in any case.").

10 *See* David S. Evans, *The Antitrust Economics of Multi-Sided Platform Markets*, 20 Yale J. on Reg. 325, 333–34 (2003); David S. Evans & Richard Schmalensee, *The Antitrust Analysis of Multi-Sided Platform Businesses, in* The Oxford Handbook of International Antitrust Economics, Volume 1 404, 409 (Roger D. Blair & D. Daniel Sokol eds., Oxford University Press, 2014) (http://doi.org/10.1093/oxfordhb/9780199859191.013.0018).

11 *See* Zachariadis & Ozcan, *supra* note 3, at 7, 10–12.

12 *See id.* at 4, 10. As mentioned before, even though FinTech startups could provide services or products while benefiting financial markets and consumers, they face challenges from incumbent banks with which the payment sector is intertwined. BigTechs, like Facebook and Amazon, however, could pose an *emerging* threat to those banks. *Id.* at 14. We contend that the threat is still *emerging*, and, in Chapter 4, we explain how the power of incumbent banks seems to be the main influence on the OB regulatory policies in Taiwan. This book focuses on how OB policies can be a game changer to new entrants in particular, such as FinTech startups, who are less capable of competing with incumbent banks than BigTechs. We acknowledge that focusing our discussion on FinTech startups

alone, rather than extending the discussion to include BigTechs, is one of this book's research limitations.

13 Nydia Remolina, *Open Banking: Regulatory Challenges for a New Form of Financial Intermediation in a Data-Driven World* 21–23 (SMU Centre for AI & Data Governance Research Paper No. 2019/05, 2019), https://ssrn.com/abstract=3475019. This commentator equates OB with BaaS, describing that "[b]oth concepts – open banking and BaaS—refer to the use of open Application Programming Interfaces that enable third parties to build applications and services around a financial institution that exposes its data and/or its infrastructure." *Id.*

14 *See* Dan Awrey & Joshua Macey, *The Promise and Perils of Open Finance* 3, 7–8 (European Corporate Governance Institute – Law Working Paper No. 632/2022; University of Chicago Coase-Sandor Institute for Law & Economics Research Paper No. 956), https://ssrn.com/abstract=4045640. Thus, in modern digital finance, the advancement and implementation of technological innovations could potentially enable non-bank FinTech firms to compete more effectively with banks owing to the latter undergoing reduction in their comparative advantage in information production. *See* Stulz, *supra* note 1, at 7.

15 Cheng-Yun Tsang, *From Industry Sandbox to Supervisory Control Box: Rethinking the Role of Regulators in the Era of FinTech*, 2019 J. L. Tech. & Pol'y 355, 371 (2019).

16 Douglas Arner, Ross Buckley, Kuzi Charamba, Dirk Zetzsche, & Artem Sergeev, *A Principle-based Approach to the Governance of BigFintechs* 4 (UN Dialog on Global Digital Finance Governance Technical Paper 3.3; University of Hong Kong Faculty of Law Research Paper No. 2021/55; UNSW Research Paper No. 21–79, 2021), https://ssrn.com/abstract=3975099.

17 *See, for example*, Andrej Savin, *The EU Digital Services Act: Towards a More Responsible Internet* 3 (Copenhagen Business School Law Research Paper Series No. 21–04, 2021), https://ssrn.com/abstract=3786792; European Commission, *The Digital Services Act Package*, https://digital-strategy.ec.europa.eu/en/policies/digital-services-act-package (last visited May 25, 2021); Sergio Gorjón, *Digital Platforms: Developments in Their Regulation and Challenges in the Financial Arena* 3–4 (Banco de España Analytical Articles No. 4/2020, 2020), https://ssrn.com/abstract=3729197; Peter Georg Picht & Heiko Richter, *Data Desiderata: On the Proposed EU Digital Services Regulation 2020*, Oxford Business Law Blog (Nov. 8, 2021), www.law.ox.ac.uk/business-law-blog/blog/2021/11/data-desiderata-proposed-eu-digital-services-regulation-2020.

18 *See* Giuseppe Colangelo & Oscar Borgogno, *Data, Innovation and Transatlantic Competition in Finance: The Case of the Access to Account Rule* 2–4 (EU L. Working Papers No. 35, 2018), https://www-cdn.law.stanford.edu/wp-content/uploads/2018/09/colangelo_borgogno_eulawwp35.pdf; Dirk Zetzsche, William A. Birdthistle, Douglas W. Arner, & Ross P. Buckley, *Digital Finance Platforms: Toward A New Regulatory Paradigm*, 23 U. Penn. J. Bus. L. 1, 56 (2020). For instance, under a platform-based business model such as the case of Uber illustrating sharing economy, it becomes debatable what the contractual relationship between platforms and service providers is. In addition, the obligations of these platforms may differ, depending on which contractual relationship between the platforms and drivers would be constituted. *See* Kim Ostergaard & Soren Sandfeld Jakobsen, *Platform Intermediaries in the Sharing Economy: Questions of Liability and Remedy*, 2019 Nordic J. Com. L. 20, 36 (2019).

19 Iris H-Y Chiu, *FinTech and Disruptive Business Models in Financial Products, Intermediation and Markets – Policy Implications for Financial Regulators*, 21 J. Tech. L. & Pol'y 55, 65 (2016).

20 *See* Colangelo & Borgogno, *supra* note 18, at 8. *See also id* (explaining that "[f]ront-end providers can offer payment initiation services ('PIS') and account information services ('AIS')."). Providers of the former services ("PISP") initiate payments on behalf of customers to give incentives and comfort to retailers in delivering the products or services; providers of the latter services provide aggregated online information regarding payment accounts to their customers who are payment service users owning the accounts. *See* Dirk A. Zetzsche, Douglas W. Arner, Ross P. Buckley, & Rolf H. Weber, *The Future of Data-Driven Finance and RegTech: Lessons from EU Big Bang II* 28–29 (EBI Working Paper Series No. 35; UNSW L. Research Series No. 19–22, 2019), https://ssrn.com/abstract=3359399; European Commission, *Payment Services Directive (PSD2): Regulatory Technical Standards (RTS) Enabling Consumers to Benefit from Safer and More Innovative Electronic Payments* 1 (Nov. 27, 2017). The end-to-end providers are platforms interacting with payers and payees, such as three-party payment firms like PayPal. Colangelo & Borgogno, *supra* note 18, at 9. In fact, if viewing the "newly emerging services providers" here in a more practical sense, they refer to the entities providing the above PIS and AIS in the context of PSD2.

21 *See* Chiu, *supra* note 19, at 65; Larry Downes & Paul Nunes, *Big-Bang Disruption*, 91 Harv. Bus. Rev. 44, 46–47 (2013). *See also* Chiu, *supra* note 19, at 111 (arguing that with the disruptive innovation framework we can study implications of FinTech innovation such as "change, substitutive potential, and structural impact," and that this framework "can inform regulators of the need to evaluate if regulatory scope is adequate, whether regulatory principles will continue to meet regulatory objectives like investor protection and financial stability, and whether regulatory rules and prescription need to update and adapt to new practices and methodologies.").

22 As for initial discussion on both BigTechs and TechFins, *see supra* note 12 and accompanying text.

23 The informational advantage is established through, for instance, the existing pool of data regarding their customers possessed by these BigTechs. *See* Jon Frost, Leonardo Gambacorta, Yi Huang, Hyun Song Shin, & Pablo Zbinden, *BigTech and the Changing Structure of Financial Intermediation* 9 (BIS Working Papers No. 779, Apr. 2019), www.bis.org/publ/work779.pdf.; Miguel de la Mano & Jorge Padilla, *Big Tech Banking*, 14 J. Competition L. & Econ. 494, 496 (2019); Stulz, *supra* note 1, at 20–21.

24 The technological advantage comes from their application of innovative technology and their accumulated technical knowledge. Frost et al., *supra* note 23, at 9; Stulz, *supra* note 1, at 20–21.

25 The reputational advantage is built on the established reputation thanks to well-known brands. *See* de la Mano & Padilla, *supra* note 23, at 496.

26 *See* Stulz, *supra* note 1, at 7.

27 *See* Chiu, *supra* note 19, at 66–67; Moran Ofir & Ido Sadeh, *More of the Same or Real Transformation: Does FinTech Warrant New Regulation?* 32–33 (2020), https://ssrn.com/abstract=3531718.

28 More on the regulatory responses in the UK and EU, that is, their OB reforms, *see* Chapter 3.

29 *See* Dan Awrey & Kristin van Zwieten, *The Shadow Payment System*, 43 J. Corp. L. 775, 777 (2018).

30 *See* Fatjon Kaja, Edoardo D. Martino, & Alessio M. Pacces, *FinTech and The Law & Economics of Disintermediation* 12–14 (ECGI Law Working Paper No. 540/2020, 2020), https://ssrn.com/abstract=3683427.

31 *See* Markus Schreiber, *Regulating Innovation, in* Law and Economics of Regulation 273, 274–75 (Klaus Mathis & Avishalon Tor eds., 2021) (http://doi.org/10.1007/978-3-030-70530-5_13).

32 *See* Section 2.3.

33 *See* Section 2.1.

34 Simonetta Vezzoso, *Fintech, Access to Data, and the Role of Competition Policy, in* Competition and Innovation 30, 33 (V. Bagnoli ed., 2018), https://dx.doi.org/10.2139/ssrn.3106594. As previously discussed, the entities participating in the payment market may include incumbent banks, BigTechs or TechFins, and FinTech startups. *See* Section 2.1.

35 *See* Vezzoso, *supra* note 34, at 33–34.

36 *See id.* at 33.

37 John Armour, Dan Awrey, Paul Davies, Luca Enriques, Jeffrey N. Gordon, Colin Mayer, & Jennifer Payne, *Principles of Financial Regulation* 62 (Oxford University Press, 2016) (http://doi.org/10.1093/acprof:oso/9780198786474.003.0017).

38 *See id.*; David T. Llewellyn, *Regulation of Retail Investment Services*, 15 Econ. Aff. 12, 13 (1995).

39 *See* Vezzoso, *supra* note 34, at 33–34.

40 *See id.*

41 *See* Chapter 1.

42 *See* Pinar Ozcan & Markos Zachariadis, *Open Banking as a Catalyst for Industry Transformation: Lessons Learned from Implementing PSD2 in Europe* 2, 5 (SWIFT Institute Working Paper, July 2021), https://ssrn.com/abstract=3984857.

43 Zetzsche et al., *supra* note 20, at 25–26.

44 Anthony I. Ogus, *Regulation: Legal Form and Economic Theory* 30 (Hart Publishing, 2004) (http://dx.doi.org/10.5040/9781472559647).

45 *See* Robert Baldwin, Martin Cave, & Martin Lodge, *Understanding Regulation: Theory, Strategy, and Practice* 13 (Oxford University Press, 1999) (http://doi.org/10.1093/acprof:osobl/9780199576081.001.0001).

46 Armour et al., *supra* note 37, at 60.

47 While we focus on the anti-competition issue in relation to the role of the incumbent banks, the reason this issue is also related to BigTech is briefly explained here. One characteristic of modern finance is that the critical resource therein is the "access to information." *See* José María Liberti & Mitchell A. Petersen, *Information: Hard and Soft*, 8 Rev. Corp. Fin. Stud. 1, 16 (2019). Mirroring this notion, as BigTech platforms specifically hold the rich data pool that they have already established, a larger amount of sale could be attained. *See* de la Mano & Padilla, *supra* note 23, at 500. Moreover, such financial alternatives might be attractive given the digital literacy of the potential consumers. *Id.* BigTech, however, could entrench themselves by way not only of their information advantages but also of the network effects that enable them to discriminate or even dominate. Competition in financial markets would thus be impaired. *See* de la Mano & Padilla, *supra* note 23, at 501–2, 507; Aluma Zernik, *The Invisible Hand, the Regulatory Touch, or the Platform's Iron Grip?* 43–44 (Nov. 20, 2019), https://ssrn.com/abstract=3490884. Scholars even argued that the OB

regulations might be particularly beneficial to BigTechs as they can more easily enter the financial industry from other industries with the aforementioned existing advantages. Ozcan & Zachariadis, *supra* note 42, at 11.

48 *See* Lawrence G. Baxter, *Betting Big: Value, Caution and Accountability in an Era of Large Banks and Complex Finance*, 31 Rev. Banking & Fin. L. 765, 831 (2012).

49 *Id.*

50 *See Banking Competition*, The World Bank, www.worldbank.org/en/publication/gfdr/gfdr-2016/background/banking-competition (last visited June 7, 2019); Deniz Anginer, Asli Demirguc-Kunt, & Min Zhu, *How Does Bank Competition Affect Systemic Stability?* 15, 17, 19 (Public Research Working Paper No. 5981, 2012), http://documents.worldbank.org/curated/en/943621468167965155/pdf/WPS5981.pdf.

51 Baxter, *supra* note 48, at 831–33.

52 *See id.*; Colangelo & Borgogno, *supra* note 18, at 14–15 (highlighting that "[i]n the light of the potential conflict of interests among TPPs and banks . . . it would not be reasonable to give banks the power of denying access to third parties[,]" and that "banks have a commercial incentive to refuse any form of cooperation with third party providers, despite the wishes of their customers and even if no justified reason could be established."); Jens-Uwe Frank & Martin Peitz, *Digital Platforms: Market Definition and Market Power*, Oxford Bus. L. Blog (May 29, 2019), www.law.ox.ac.uk/business-law-blog/blog/2019/05/digital-platforms-market-definition-and-market-power (noting that "[b]arriers to entry are at the core of persistent market power and, thus, the entrenchment of incumbent platforms."). For analysis of the difficulties with access to information faced by new FinTech startups in Taiwan, see Chapter 4.

53 *See* Chang-Hsien Tsai, *To Regulate or Not to Regulate? A Comparison of Government Responses to Peer-to-Peer Lending among the United States, China, and Taiwan*, 87 U. Cin. L. Rev. 1077, 1121 (2019). When it comes to the traditional view of trade-off between facilitating a competitive financial system and concerns of prudential regulation, a competition law scholar emphasizes that "[r]egulators are ambivalent about truly promoting competition in the financial sector," that "[p]rudential regulators in particular think in terms of trade-offs between competition and stability," and that "[i]n this popular view, restrictions on competition would improve banks' profitability, reduce failure rates and hence safeguard stability." Arnoud W. A. Boot, *Financial Services: Consolidation and Strategic Positioning, in* The International Handbook of Competition 133, 160 (Manfred Neumann & Jürgen Weigand eds., Edward Elgar Publishing, 2004) (https://doi.org/10.4337/9781845423520.00010).

54 *See* Tsai, *supra* note 53, at 1118–21. We will delve into this organizational issue regarding the design of financial regulators' structure. *See* Chapter 3, Section 1.3 and Chapter 5, Section 1.

55 *See* Section 2.1.

56 *See* Section 2.2.

57 *See* Chapter 3.

58 *See* Fabiana Di Porto & Gustavo Ghidini, *'I Access Your Data You Access Mine': Requiring Data Reciprocity in Payment Services*, 51 Int'L Rev. Intell. Prop. & Competition L. 307 (2020), https://ssrn.com/abstract=3407294.

59 Colangelo & Borgogno, *supra* note 18, at 25.

60 *Id.*

61 *See* Di Porto & Ghidini, *supra* note 58, at 8.

62 For instance, there might be a conflict between regulation and innovation due to fears of liability for unknown risks. *See* Michael Faure, Louis Visscher, & Franziska Weber, *Liability for Unknown Risks: A Law and Economics Perspective*, 7 J. Eur. Tort L. 198, 211–12 (2016).

63 *See, for example,* Zetzsche et al., *supra* note 20, at 38; Mark Fenwick, Wulf A. Kaal & Erik P. M. Vermeulen, *Regulation Tomorrow: What Happens When Technology Is Faster than the Law?* 6 Am. U. Bus. L. Rev. 561, 573 (2017).

64 Sofia Ranchordás & Mattis van't Schip, *Future-Proofing Legislation for the Digital Age*, *in* Time, Law, and Change: An Interdisciplinary Study 347, 356 (Sofia Ranchordás & Yaniv Roznai eds., Hart Publishing, 2017) (http://dx.doi.org/10.5040/9781509930968.ch-016). These scholars applied the concept of responsive regulation that we mentioned before to the regulation of innovation. *Id.* at 354. A discussion on the application of responsive regulation could also be found in the context of financial regulation, *see* Mariusz J. Golecki, *Regulation and Deregulation of Financial Markets from the Perspective of Law and Economics*, *in* Law and Economics of Regulation 233, 237–39 (Klaus Mathis & Avishalon Tor eds., 2021) (http://doi.org/10.1007/978-3-030-70530-5_11).

65 *See, for example*, Cristie Ford, *Making Regulation Robust in the Innovation Era* 12–13 (2021), https://ssrn.com/abstract=3839865.

66 *See id.* at 5. It is even argued that we cannot just expect to bolster innovation via regulation in a general sense, "without understanding the innovation in question, how it is diffusing, who benefits from its adoption, what unanticipated consequences may flow from it, and especially how it could undermine, circumvent, or otherwise neutralize existing regulatory processes and priorities." *Id.* at 6.

67 *Id.* at 7.

68 *See* Section 2.2.2.

69 *See, for example*, Ford, *supra* note 65, at 12–13.

70 *See* Tsai, *supra* note 53, at 1082.

3 Experiences of the EU and the UK in Advocating Open Banking

In Chapter 2, we examined the regulatory issues concerning the rise of new market participants in the payment sector. Our examination revealed the frictions among information, innovation, and regulation in the modern financial markets as well as the role of regulators to minimize these frictions. In this chapter, we turn to the actual regulatory responses to those regulatory issues discussed in the previous chapter. In particular, we focus on the role of regulators when addressing these issues by investigating what the appropriate institutional design of financial regulators should be in order to promote financial competition and innovation in the modern digital finance.[1]

Accordingly, this chapter embarks on a study of the regulators' role in the modern financial markets by examining the OB-promoting regulatory regimes in the EU and the UK. As the OB regulatory reforms in both the UK and the EU represent a more comprehensive and programmatic approach, their experiences provide lessons for other markets such as Taiwan, which is currently initiating such a reform.[2] Section 1 introduces the ideology of OB reforms in the UK and the EU. Section 2 explains the regulatory strategies of OB in the UK and the EU based on seven features.[3] Section 3 summarizes the findings of the study.

1. Ideology of Open Banking

1.1 Path to Smart Regulation Underlying the PSD2 Development

There is no single, easy regulatory approach to addressing the issues arising in the age of FinTech. Literature about regulatory responses to FinTech have centered on, for instance, whether to regulate FinTech either before or after the development and deployment of it.[4] Regulatory approaches to FinTech

DOI: 10.4324/9781003126324-3

in different jurisdictions vary widely—including doing nothing, allowing a certain number of FinTech activities on a case-by-case basis, interpreting existing regulations, creating the "sandbox" regime, and enacting new regulations.[5] Though regulation has associated costs,[6] and doing nothing might be free at the outset, that approach could become problematic—especially when financial innovation evolves.[7] The costs of doing nothing may become apparent when a laissez-faire regulatory approach, rather than rigorous regulation, is adopted in some jurisdictions where financial innovation is flourishing in its infancy.[8] This approach, according to commentators, may underestimate the need for regulating when financial innovation is fast developing.[9] Nevertheless, such a lax regulatory approach to, for instance, the platform economy, has been altered, tightened, and tuned to be stricter.[10]

In the sphere of OB, however, the selection of regulatory approaches goes beyond the dichotomy between a hands-on and hands-off regulatory approach. An appropriate design of regulation would realize the benefits associated with the fact that a diversification of market participants can be witnessed.[11] In particular, PSD2, which is the regulatory approach to fostering OB to bring benefits to the markets, was recognized by commentators as an instance of a "smart regulation"; this approach re-balances regulatory objectives rather than merely implementing regulatory burdens.[12]

1.2 Historical Background of PSD2

After an initial reflection on PSD2 from a "smart" regulation perspective, this section dives into the historical background of PSD2. From a broader perspective, OB regulatory reforms are of vital importance insofar as the regulations would be capable of disrupting the financial industry significantly.[13] With respect to information sharing between banks and other parties, OB has been deemed the ultimate catalyst for information sharing in different sectors of the economy, creating larger impacts.[14]

As discussed before, modern financial markets have witnessed transformations thanks to, among other things, the rise of new market participants.[15] Given this phenomenon, the question of how to re-balance innovation and competition with traditional regulatory objectives of financial safety and soundness in payment markets has garnered EU regulators' attention for more than a decade.[16] Some have noted that this issue has been partly addressed by the EU regulators' efforts to "reengineer" the EU-level payment system.[17] PSD2 is an example of such efforts to facilitate transactions where new categories of nonbank payment service providers are involved, while strengthening consumer protection.[18] Thus, after the PSD2 proposal in June 2013, the EU enacted PSD2 on January 12, 2016 and set a deadline of January 13, 2018, for member states to implement it into their national laws.[19] PSD2 was the first regulation to make banks' data-sharing mandatory.[20] It is based on the success of PSD1,[21] which established a framework to harmonize payment transactions, integrate the European market, and address, in particular, the technological innovation adopted in the payment sector.[22] PSD2 aims to simplify and facilitate transactions on the basis of information about customers' accounts, as well as to achieve the aforementioned goals by requiring coordination between traditional banks (where the customers' accounts are housed) and the third-party providers (TPPs) of payment services; TPPs include payment initiation services providers (PISPs) and account information services providers (AISPs).[23]

A similar regulatory trajectory has also appeared in the UK since a report was published by the Competition and Markets Authority (CMA), identifying the entry barriers in the banking sector. Advocacy for the UK's OB initiative was reflected in the CMA's findings on barriers to entry and expansion in retail banking.[24] Specifically, the Payment Services Regulations 2017 (PSRs 2017) was implemented to transpose PSD2 into the UK.[25] Given the growing need for regulation due to the growth in technological innovation, problems such as legal uncertainty, potential security risks, and the lack of consumer protection could arise.[26] Therefore, both PSD2 and the UK's OB aim to enable the new payment means to broaden the market and to increase efficiency of the payment system. Meanwhile consumer protection is ensured "by means of increasing transparency, efficiency[,] and security of retail payments (e.g., stricter authentication mechanisms) as well as allocating obligations and liabilities to the involved stakeholders."[27] Against this backdrop, the concept undergirding PSD2 is based on data portability and control, which enables customers to control their data stored in banks' data pools, thereby sharing the data from banks to TPPs based on customers' consent.[28]

1.3 Regulators' Role in Promoting Open Banking

Prior studies discussed OB regulatory reforms in the UK and the EU from different perspectives.[29] This section focuses on the role of regulators in those reforms. In general, those OB reforms are built to mitigate the financial market's anticompetition tendencies by lowering the barriers emerging market participants face, so as to elevate competition.[30] Those regulatory reforms, most importantly, illustrate a compulsory approach given the potential unwillingness of banks to otherwise open or release customers' data they have been collecting.[31] In effect, while information plays a critical role in modern digital finance, sharing information between institutions through regulatory compulsion has been deemed to be more effective.[32]

As the approach is by and large compulsory, three matters (discussed subsequently) regarding the role of regulators may arise.

First, compulsory regulation might trigger the need to establish an independent and powerful authority to deal exclusively with specific issues in modern finance. A regulatory trajectory on which diversified tasks or even competing responsibilities are assigned to a single authority may not be suitable in modern finance where complex issues arise with mission conflicts during the authority's fulfillment of those tasks.[33] Therefore, in order to establish an independent authority, which is responsible for specific issues such as ensuring competition and fostering innovation, we can either place it under an existing authority given minimal institutional change, or create a brand new authority that is separate from a naturally conservative prudential regulator.[34]

Second, given the potential volume and complexity of regulatory issues arising from financial competition and innovation, different authorities might have concurrent and overlapping powers. Therefore, coordination and collaboration between these different authorities, that is, co-regulation, are of vital significance.[35] The coordination between different national authorities such as sector regulators and competition regulators is especially important in digital finance as mandates and practices of those regulators may not be compatible when it comes to complementary regulation of legal issues in digital finance.[36] These considerations with respect to the establishment of a specialized and professional authority and the collaboration between different authorities are reflected, to an extent, in the OB experience in the UK.[37]

Last but not least, financial markets have been undergoing digital transformations, leading to the formation of modern digital finance where innovative technologies or business models emerge. These phenomena reflect that contemporary FinTech regulation should be flexible and dynamic in order to adapt to the rapid evolution and increasing complexity of financial markets.[38] A more adaptive regulatory approach together with an adaptive institutional design of regulatory authorities are capable of responding to the changes in the markets more aptly.[39]

In the following sections, we look into the OB regulations' toolkit in the UK and the EU with respect to seven features by emphasizing how OB is promoted through a mandatory or compulsory approach.[40] Those features include the following: (1) what is the regulatory manner? (2) Who should open the data? (3) Who may access the data? (4) What is the scope of the data to be opened? (5) Who may decide on the type of the data to be opened? (6) Who may decide on the API standards? (7) How to govern the third-party providers? In addition, the role played by regulators based on the aforementioned features will be studied respectively.

2. Regulatory Reforms of Open Banking in the UK and the EU

2.1 Seven Features of the UK's and the EU's Regulatory Reforms

2.1.1 Compulsory Approach: Complementary Regulation Beyond Traditional Financial Regulators

The OB reforms in the UK and the EU are promoted through a compulsory regulatory approach, whereas, as mentioned before, in other jurisdictions OB may be promoted through mere encouragement.[41] The UK's OB, which transplanted PSD2 into its local context, is mandated and regulated by such regulators as the CMA, which serves a proactive role in leading OB,[42] as well as the Financial Conduct Authority (FCA), which regulates the financial services providers (including AISP and/or PISP) who could access the data.[43] PSD2 is implemented mainly through the PSRs 2017 in the UK.[44] Given the difficulties confronted by new market participants, such as smaller and newer banks and other nonbank entities that provide financial services, the CMA implemented OB so as to help these new market participants access data.[45] In 2016, to put OB into practice, the CMA established a company named the OBIE.[46] The OBIE operates as an independent entity to carry out orders from the CMA.[47] The OBIE is funded by the nine financial institutions (also known as "CMA9") that are mandated to develop OB under instructions from the CMA.[48] In addition, the OBIE's governance, composition, and budget are decided by the CMA.[49] As a result, the OBIE, which is a nonprofit private company limited by guarantee without share capital,[50] seems to have both private and public characteristics as it is funded by the aforementioned private entities while being subject to governmental control. As the governmental body (i.e., the CMA) delegates part of its regulatory power to the OBIE, this private entity acquires some public nature to implement public policies. This type of entity exemplifies the quasi-public regulator deemed suitable for implementing FinTech-related policies.[51]

This compulsory approach contrasts with the voluntary and self-regulatory approach adopted in other jurisdictions such as Taiwan.[52] Specifically, under the UK's "twin-peak" regulatory system,[53] there are two implications concerning the implementation of OB via co-regulation by both the CMA and the FCA, that is, coordination and collaboration between these two authorities to produce complementary outcomes. On the one hand, in terms of advocating competition, the establishment of the CMA in 2014 reflects the need for a single powerful voice to promote competition for the benefit of consumers as it combined two competition authorities, the Office of Fair Trading (OFT) and the Competition Commission (CC).[54]

The creation of a single competition authority is expected to generate benefits from its faster and less burdensome operation.[55] Improving competition in the markets by implementing OB has been one of CMA's main missions.[56] Moreover, although OB centers on the data sharing, the establishment of CMA and its leading role in OB were regarded as an early reflection of the future data economy.[57] On the other hand, the CMA and FCA hold concurrent and overlapping powers with respect to the implementation of the UK's OB. While the CMA and OBIE (established by the CMA) are implementing OB as described earlier, the FCA is, to an extent, also implementing OB by providing guidance.[58] Nevertheless, the concurrent and overlapping powers are leveraged, on the basis of the complementary resources of these two authorities, thereby implementing OB more effectively with such co-regulation or complementary regulation.[59] Such collaboration depends on a strong dialog between the CMA and the FCA with "specific tools such as conduct regulation, supervision[,] and enforcement."[60]

2.1.2 Parties Who Should Open Data

In both the UK and the EU, the primary regulated parties are the account servicing payment service providers (the "ASPSPs" or the "payment service provider providing and maintaining a payment account for a payer" as defined in PSD2).[61] The ASPSPs are primarily banks, and the requirements to open their data pool turn them into "involuntary 'platform as a service' (PaaS) providers for disruptive FinTech start-ups seeking to disintermediate them."[62] In the UK, the parties who are mandated by the CMA to open their APIs are CMA9, while other entities can opt in as voluntary API providers.[63] As discussed earlier, in the UK, those CMA9 banks are involved in the formation and operation of the OBIE, the entity leading OB.[64] Nonetheless, it seems that the CMA9 are neither the sole parties involved in the operation of the OBIE nor those deciding who the beneficiaries are. For instance, as the operation of the OBIE is subject to the CMA,[65] there is a certain process through which the recipients of data are decided.[66] As stated in the operation guidelines of the OBIE, there were extensive collaboration and consultation with "TPP communities" and "prominent FinTech leaders" when the OBIE Standard were being formulated.[67] As discussed here, whether the TPPs could participate in the OB is neither solely decided by the CMA9 nor by the OBIE. Rather, a clear and transparent process is applied.[68]

2.1.3 Parties Who May Access Data

The aims of OB in the UK and the EU are to grant access to customers' account information to PISPs and AISPs.[69] Under the PSD2 framework, this is referred to as the "access to account" rule (the "XS2A" rule).[70] Under this rule, FinTech startups could be the beneficiaries of the rule when they serve as PISPs or AISPs.[71] The aims could be achieved by, for example, creating and implementing open common APIs. In the UK, these measures are mandated via the OBIE's creating a set of open API specifications and OB standards.[72] Therefore, those mandatory specifications and standards contribute to the higher level of "compulsory APIs standardization" in the UK;[73] this is crucial to both spurring innovation and protecting consumers.[74] In addition, in the UK, the scope of regulated third parties who could obtain access to data may be broader than payment service providers (PSPs) authorized under PSD2 (including PISPs and AISPs) because of the "whitelisting" process, by which the CMA grants access to those third parties.[75] For instance, even though the price-comparison websites (PCWs) are considered by the CMA to fall outside the scope of specific institutions under PSD2, they may be permitted to access data through CMA's whitelisting.[76]

The OBIE is charged with controlling and maintaining the OB Directory, which provides the whitelist of regulated parties allowed to operate in the OB Ecosystem.[77] The TPPs that wish to enroll in the UK's OB should follow a process in which the regulators play an important role. First, the TPPs should be regulated by the FCA; second, they could choose to enroll in the OB Directory; third, their services will be tested in the Directory Sandbox; fourth, they could launch their services after their regulatory permissions are confirmed by the FCA.[78] Accordingly, the FCA performs a crucial part in determining whether and how their services (e.g., AISP, PISP or both) fall into the regulatory definitions of the UK's OB.[79]

2.1.4 Scope of Data to Be Opened

PSD2 and the UK's OB oblige ASPSPs (including banks and building societies) to give access to customers' account information, excluding "sensitive payment data."[80] To both AISPs and PISPs, the name of the account owner or payer (the payment service user, PSU) and the PSU's account number are accessible and can be displayed through the API notwithstanding.[81]

2.1.5 Who Decides the Type and Scope of Data to Be Opened?

Under the regulator-led model of OB in the UK and the EU, the details, which include the scope of data or the type of data that should be excluded, are determined according to the corresponding regulations and rules.[82] The regulators play an important role in the supervision of regulated parties and the implementation of the regulations. For example, in the UK, compliance with the regulations under which "sensitive payment data" should be excluded largely relies on the supervision of the FCA.[83] In the context of PSD2, payment service providers should develop mechanisms mitigating the operational and security risks and provide the assessment of those mechanisms to competent authorities in member states.[84] In particular, according to the guidelines issued by the European Banking Authority (EBA), such mechanisms should include measures dealing with security issues regarding sensitive data.[85] Thus, it could be observed that public authorities play a crucial role when it comes to the issues regarding sensitive data.

2.1.6 Who Decides on API Standards?

The delivery of OB inevitably involves setting some technical standards, which may be complex.[86] Such standardization is not mandated by PSD2, however. Instead, PSD2 creates a regulatory framework by requiring the alignment between account access and the requirements made by the EBA under the Regulatory Technical Standards (RTS).[87] PSD2 appears to be quite flexible as it leaves open the details of APIs, and does not require the establishment of common API standards.[88] Regardless, as explained before, the EBA drafted and published the RTS in order to establish a framework for the cooperation and exchange of information between competent authorities under the PSD2.[89] On the contrary, in the UK, the CMA required nine banks to place "the Open Banking Standard in collaboration with representatives of third parties and members representing the interests of consumers and [small- and medium-sized enterprises ('SMEs')]."[90] Therefore, without the mandate of common API standards, the level of standardization in the EU appears to be lower than that within the UK due to the less prescriptive regulatory approach in the former.[91] Standardization is thus still an issue in the EU as it is pivotal to harmonization and efficient data sharing.[92]

2.1.7 Who Governs or Supervises Third-party Providers?

In line with the regulator-led approach to OB in the UK and the EU, TPPs that can participate in OB are required to register with or be authorized by competent authorities such as the FCA.[93] Regulators thus play a crucial role in ensuring compliance with the regulations promoting OB.[94] In addition, in order to bring more TPPs under the scope of OB, the regulatory strategies in the UK and the EU provide more leniency or additional proportionality for AISPs and PISPs.[95] Such measures, according to a consultation paper released by the EBA when developing guidelines for them, are expected to bring more choices for consumers and establish equal conditions for competition.[96]

2.2 *Comparison of Open Banking Regulations Between the UK and the EU*

The earlier discussions on OB regulations in the UK and the EU are compared and summarized in Table 3.1. To furnish a more holistic comparative study, in the next chapter this table will be expanded to include OB regulatory policies in Taiwan.[97]

Table 3.1 A Comparison of the Open Banking Regulations in the UK and the EU.

	UK	*EU*
Mandatory or voluntary?	• Compulsory	• Compulsory
Who should open the data?	• ASPSPs	• ASPSPs
Who may access the data?	• PISPs & AISPs • A broad range of additional third parties—through the process of "whitelisting"	• PISPs & AISPs
What is the scope of the data to be opened?	• Account information	• Account information
Who decides the type and scope of the data to be opened?	• Exclusions of data to be opened largely depends on the FCA.	• Assessment of the mechanisms protecting sensitive data should be provided to competent authorities in member states. • Guidelines on the above assessment were issued by the EBA.
Who decides on the API standards?	• Co-determination by both CMA9 and "representatives of third parties and members representing the interests of consumers and SMEs." • Open Banking Standard is adopted.	• No mandate for the establishment of common API standards. • EBA drafted the RTS.
How to govern or supervise TPPs?	• PISPs should be authorized and AISPs should be registered. • They are regulated by the FCA, providing more leniency or additional proportionality for AISPs and PISPs.	• PISPs should be authorized and AISPs should be registered. • They are regulated by competent authorities in member states, providing more leniency or additional proportionality for AISPs and PISPs.

Source: the Authors

3. Conclusion

This chapter explored the regulations promoting and mandating OB in the UK and the EU. These regulations are worth examining because the PSD2 was also regarded as an OB development model for other jurisdictions.[98] Both the UK's OB initiative and PSD2, which realize the idea of OB, were deemed groundbreaking as they encourage competition in the financial markets by creatively focusing on information sharing.[99] As a whole, the introduction of OB and the regulations thereof mirror an establishment of a future ecosystem that centers on information.[100]

As reported, in early 2021, the OB development in the UK was deemed successful and efficient as over three million UK consumers and companies could use the products enabled by the OB policy, and innovation and competition have accordingly been fostered.[101] As the UK's OB transposes PSD2 into its local legal regime, its regulatory design concretely shows how a mandatory approach could be realized. We made the analysis of this mandatory approach based on seven features by, among others, revealing the regulators' role in implementing OB. This mandatory approach helps and facilitates information sharing.[102] As shown before, regulators play an influential part in delivering OB in each feature of mandating OB. Most importantly, the first key to such a successful regulatory design would be the establishment of a professional authority independently handling competition issues, like the CMA. Then, under the CMA, the OBIE is created to implement OB policies in the UK. The second key is the effective collaboration between the existing sectoral regulator, that is, the FCA, and the regulator "striving to smooth technological innovation and competition" through antitrust enforcement,[103] that is, the CMA. The collaboration between the FCA and CMA matters since both are, to a certain extent, leading and mandating OB. In the next chapter, we inquire into the OB regulation in Taiwan and compare it with its counterparts in the EU and the UK.

Notes

1 *See, e.g.*, Yueh-Ping Yang & Chen-Yun Tsang, *RegTech and the New Era of Financial Regulators: Envisaging More Public-Private-Partnership Models of Financial Regulators*, 21 U. Pa. J. Bus. L. 354, 371–72 (2018); Samuel N. Weinstein, *Financial Regulation in the (Receding) Shadow of Antitrust*, 91 Temp. L. Rev. 447, 452 (2019); Rory Van Loo, *Rise of Digital Regulator*, 66 Duke L. J. 1267, 1274 (2017); Rachel E. Barkow, *Insulating Agencies: Avoiding Capture Through Institutional Design*, 89 Tex. L. Rev. 15, 19 (2010).

2 Alessio Botta, Nunzio Digiacomo, Reinhard Höll, & Liz Oakes, *PSD2: Taking Advantages of Open-Banking Disruption*, McKinsey & Company (Jan. 2018), www.mckinsey.com/industries/financial-services/our-insights/psd2-taking-advantage-of-open-banking-disruption.

3 The comparison study between the UK/EU strategies and those of Taiwan would also entail an analysis based on these seven features. *See* Chapter 4, Section 2.

4 *See, e.g.*, Dirk A. Zetzsche, Ross P. Buckley, Jànos N. Barberis, & Douglas W. Arner, *Regulating a Revolution: From Regulatory Sandboxes to Smart Regulation*, 23 Fordham J. Corp. & Fin. L. 31, 50 (2017).

5 *See id.* at 44–46.

6 In relation to financial innovation, "the inhibition of technical change" is one of the indirect costs of regulation. Anthony I. Ogus, *Regulation: Legal Form and Economic Theory* 155 (Hart Publishing, 2004) (http://dx.doi.org/10.5040/9781472559647).

7 The costs of doing nothing in the context of regulating the payment industry could include systemic risks that affect society at large. *See* Dan Awrey & Kristin van Zwieten, *The Shadow Payment System*, 43 J. Corp. L. 775, 809 (2018).

8 For instance, a so-called "Zen approach" was adopted during the infancy of Chinese FinTech development. *See* Zetzsche et al., *supra* note 4, at 50–51.

9 *See id.* The case made by commentators to explain how the "Zen" (i.e., doing nothing) approach fails to foresee the need to regulate is the money market fund issued by Alibaba Group in China. *Id.*

10 A scholar observed that this transition is happening in China. Angela Huyue Zhang, *Agility Over Stability: China's Great Reversal in Regulating the Platform Economy*, 63 Har. Int'l L. J. (forthcoming, 2022), at 26–28, https://ssrn.com/abstract=3892642.

11 *See* Zetzsche et al., *supra* note 4, at 91 (arguing that "a sandbox should be accompanied by an appropriately designed system of forbearance, dispensation, and restricted licensing, or other tools of smart regulation, such as a well-designed piloting framework or sandbox umbrella . . . ."); Hamish Thomas, Anita Kimber, & Wayne Brown, *How Regulation is Unlocking the Potential of Open Banking in the UK*, EY (Mar. 28, 2019), www.ey.com/en_gl/banking-capital-markets/how-regulation-is-unlocking-the-potential-of-open-banking-in-the-uk.

12 *See* Zetzsche et al., *supra* note 4, at 56 (noting that "PSD2 is important because it goes beyond merely adding new elements to an existing framework but rather attempts to transform the sector through technology—an example of the sort of smart regulation . . . ."). *See also id.* at 58 (highlighting that "the United Kingdom provides an example of a jurisdiction which has altered the mandate of its regulator to require considerations of innovation and economic competitiveness in regulatory decisions."). The term "smart regulation" in the context of financial regulation was deemed to be more relevant to re-balancing different regulatory objectives. For these objectives, *see id.* at 31 (describing "[f]inancial regulators increasingly seek to balance the traditional regulatory objectives of financial stability and consumer protection with promoting growth and innovation."). To be clear, the concept of "re-balanced regulatory objectives," involving the idea of striking a balance among promoting innovation, ensuring financial stability, and protecting consumers, implicitly envisages the mitigation of the frictions among innovation, information, and regulation. *See id.* at 100. Additionally, in the context of financial regulation, "smart regulation" involves sequencing and combining different regulatory tools as a strategy that is often used to regulate FinTech. *See id.* at 91–92, 98. It was further suggested that the tools used to regulate FinTech should be proportionate to, for instance, the size of the firms. *See id.* at 94. As discussed above, the concepts of smart regulation proposed and cultivated by Gunningham, Grabosky,

and Sinclair could be found in the context of financial regulation and FinTech. In nature, smart regulation originally "refers to a form of regulatory pluralism that embraces flexible, imaginative and innovative forms of social control" and "harnesses governments as well as business and third parties." Neil Gunningham & Darren Sinclair, *Smart Regulation, in* Regulatory Theory: Foundations and Applications 133, 133 (Peter Drahos ed., Australian National University Press, 2017) (http://doi.org/10.22459/RT.02.2017.08). In addition to featuring the participants in the process of regulation, another important part of smart regulation involves implementing complementary combinations of social controls or policy tools. *Id.* at 133–34, 139.

13 *See* Zetzsche et al., *supra* note 4, at 56 (emphasizing that "PSD2 is expected to fundamentally change the payments value chain, business profitability, and customer expectations.").

14 *See* Linda Jeng, *Inception to Open Banking, in* Open Banking 1, 3–4, 6 (Linda Jeng ed., Oxford University Press, 2022) (http://doi.org/10.1093/oso/9780197582879.003.0001).

15 *See* Chapter 2, Section 2.1.

16 Jane K. Winn, *Reengineering European Payment Law* 2 (June 30, 2019), https://ssrn.com/abstract=3412457.

17 *See id.* at 2–3.

18 *See id.* at 4.

19 EY, *The Revised Payment Services Directive (PSD2): What You Need to Know* 1–2 (2018), www.ey.com/Publication/vwLUAssets/Regulatory_agenda_updates_PSDII_Luxembourg/$FILE/Regulatory%20agenda%20updates_PSDII_Lux.pdf.

20 Douglas W. Arner, Ross. P. Buckley, & Dirk Zetzsche, *Open Banking, Open Data, and Open Finance: Lessons from the European Union, in* Open Banking 147, 148 (Linda Jeng ed., Oxford University Press, 2022) (http://doi.org/10.1093/oso/9780197582879.003.0009).

21 Directive 2007/64/EC of the European Parliament and of the Council of 13 November 2007 on Payment Services in the Internal Market Amending Directives 97/7/EC, 2002/65/EC, 2005/60/EC and 2006/48/EC and Repealing Directive 97/5/EC, 2007 O.J. (L 319) 1 [hereinafter Directive 2007/64/EC].

22 Directive 2015/2366, Amending Directives 2002/65/EC, 2009/110/EC and 2013/36/EU and Regulation (EU) No 1093/2010, and Repealing Directive 2007/64/EC, 2015 O.J. (L 337) 35, recital 3, at 36 [hereinafter Directive 2015/2366]; Winn, *supra* note 16, at 4, 22.

23 *See id.* at 27–28. Both the PISPs and AISPs are front-end payment service providers furnishing services that enable payment service users to initiate payment orders and to view their financial situation. Giuseppe Colangelo & Oscar Borgogno, *Data, Innovation and Transatlantic Competition in Finance: The Case of the Access to Account Rule* 8–9 (EU L. Working Papers No. 35, 2018), https://www-cdn.law.stanford.edu/wp-content/uploads/2018/09/colangelo_borgogno_eulawwp35.pdf. PISPs are the service providers who can transfer the payments between consumers and merchants. The payers can therefore make payments without opening bank accounts with the PISPs but instruct them to process the debit transactions; these transactions against the payees are then directly charged to the payers' bank accounts. Sofort, which is a German FinTech startup, and iDeal, which is a collaborative initiative among several Dutch banks, are the examples of PISPs. Winn, *supra* note 16, at 27. AISPs are the account data

aggregators who can collect and integrate the data of different banks accounts. Mint in the US and Money Dashboard in the UK exemplify this type of service provider. *Id.* at 26.

24 CMA, *Retail Banking Market Investigation: Final Report* xxxi (Aug. 9, 2016), https://assets.publishing.service.gov.uk/media/57ac9667e5274a0f6c00007a/retail-banking-market-investigation-full-final-report.pdf.

25 Explanatory Memorandum to the Payment Services Regulations 2017 No. 752 ¶ 2.1; The Payment Services Regulations 2017, SI 2017/752.

26 Directive 2015/2366, *supra* note 22, recital 4, at 36. *See also* Mark Fenwick, Wulf A. Kaal, & Erik P. M. Vermeulen, *Regulation Tomorrow: What Happens When Technology Is Faster than the Law?* 6 Am. U. Bus. L. Rev. 561, 573 (2017) (noting that as technology is still in its early stage, unaddressed regulatory issues could inhibit innovation).

27 EY, *supra* note 19, at 3; Directive 2015/2366, *supra* note 22, recital 6, at 36.

28 *See, e.g.,* Cristina Poncibó & Oscar Borgogno, *Law and Autonomous Systems Series: The Day After Tomorrow of Banking – On FinTech, Data Control and Consumer Empowerment*, Oxford Bus. L. Blog (Apr. 5, 2018), www.law.ox.ac.uk/business-law-blog/blog/2018/04/law-and-autonomous-systems-series-day-after-tomorrow-banking-fintech; Xiang-Bo Huang (黃相博), *Ren Gong Zhi Hui Zai Jin Rong Ye De Ying Yong—Lun Shu Wei Jin Rong Yu Yi Ban Ge Ren Zi Liao Bao Hu Gui Ze Zhi Shi Yong Yu Chong Tu* (人工智慧在金融業的應用—論數位金融與一般個人資料保護規則之適用與衝突) [*The Application of Artificial Intelligence in Financial Industry – A Study on Digital Finance and the Applicability and Conflicts of GDPR*], *in* Fa Lü Si Wei Yu Zhi Du De Zhi Hui Zhuan Xing (法律思維與制度的智慧轉型) [Smart Transitions of Legal Thinking and Institutions] 385, 399 (Jian-Liang Li (李建良) ed., Yuan-Zhao Publishing (元照出版社), 2020).

29 For instance, some studies introduced important rules such as the access-to-account rule set under PSD2 and other fundamental concepts therein. *See, e.g.,* Colangelo & Borgogno, *supra* note 23, at 14–18. In addition, other literature examined PSD2 based on its content and further linked it with other concepts; for example, the work of Zetzsche et al. described fundamental properties of PSD2 and explained the impact it brought in the belief that it contributes to the formation of a data-driven finance. Dirk A. Zetzsche, Douglas W. Arner, Ross P. Buckley, & Rolf H. Weber, *The Future of Data-Driven Finance and RegTech: Lessons from EU Big Bang II* 31–32 (EBI Working Paper Series No. 35; UNSW L. Research Series No. 19–22, 2019), https://ssrn.com/abstract=3359399. Other commentators illustrated a so-called "API economy" in relation to the introduction of open banking. *See* Markos Zachariadis & Pinar Ozcan, *The API Economy and Digital Transformation in Financial Services: The Case of Open Banking* 2, 4–5 (SWIFT Inst. Working Paper No. 2016–001, June 15, 2017), https://ssrn.com/abstract=2975199.

30 *See e.g.,* Zetzsche et al., *supra* note 29, at 25; Miguel de la Mano & Jorge Padilla, *Big Tech Banking*, 14 J. Competition L. & Econ. 494, 503 (2019); Arnoud W. A. Boot, *The Future of Banking: From Scale & Scope Economics to Fintech*, *in* FinTech and Banking. Friends or Foes? 77, 89–90 (Giorgio Barba, Giacomo Calzolari, & Alberto Franco Pozzolo eds., Europeye srl, 2017), http://european-economy.eu/wp-content/uploads/2018/01/EE_2.2017-2.pdf. *See also* Fernando Zunzunegui, *Digitalisation of Payment Services* 24–25 (Ibero-American Institute for Law and Finance Working Paper Series 5/2018, 2018), https://ssrn.com/

abstract=3256281 (noting that "the financial crisis has damaged the banks' reputation," that "[a]gainst this background, the European Union has opted to open up payment services to promote competition and innovation," and that "PSD2 brings about the definitive opening up of the payment market to third parties other than the banks.").

31 *See Open Banking Year One: Insights from the CMA9 and More*, Finextra (Jan. 11, 2019), www.finextra.com/newsarticle/33194/open-banking-year-one-insights-from-the-cma9-and-more; Nydia Remolina, *Open Banking: Regulatory Challenges for a New Form of Financial Intermediation in a Data-Driven World* 40 (SMU Centre for AI & Data Governance Research Paper No. 2019/05, 2019), https://ssrn.com/abstract=3475019.

32 Cheng-Yun Tsang, *From Industry Sandbox to Supervisory Control Box: Rethinking the Role of Regulators in the Era of FinTech*, 2019 J. L. Tech. & Pol'y 355, 374 (2019).

33 Chang-Hsien Tsai, *To Regulate or Not to Regulate? A Comparison of Government Responses to Peer-to-Peer Lending among the United States, China, and Taiwan*, 87 U. Cin. L. Rev. 1077, 1120 (2019); Rory Van Loo, *Making Innovation More Competitive: The Case of FinTech*, 65 UCLA L. Rev. 232, 269 (2018).

34 *See* Van Loo, *supra* note 33, at 275–76.

35 Similar concepts were presented in the research on the sharing economy in the United States, arguing that regional governance should aim to complement statewide regulations, forming "the state and local partnership in the regulation of the sharing economy" when a regional identity and home rules are desired. Janice C. Griffith, *Role of State Governments in the Sharing Economy*, in Cambridge Handbook on Law and Regulation of the Sharing Economy 231, 245–46 (Nestor Davidson, Michèle Finck, & John Infranca eds., Cambridge University Press, 2018) (http://doi.org/10.1017/9781108255882.018).

36 Remolina, *supra* note 31, at 46–47; *see also,* Chapter 2.

37 *See* Section 2.1.1.

38 *See, e.g.,* Andrew W. Lo, *Regulatory Reform in the Wake of the Financial Crisis of 2007–2008*, 1 J. Fin. Econ. Pol'y 4, 7 (2009). Regarding the adaptability debate of civil law and common law bifurcation of legal origins, *see* Chang-Hsien Tsai, Ching-Fu Lin, & Han-Wei Liu, *The Diffusion of the Sandbox Approach to Disruptive Innovation and Its Limitations*, 53 Cornell Int'l L. J. 261, 280–81.

39 *See* Lawrence G. Baxter, *Adaptive Regulation in the Amoral Bazaar*, 128 S. Afr. L. J. 253, 264–66 (2011).

40 *See* Section 2.1.

41 *See, e.g.,* Han-Wei Liu, *Two Decades of Laws and Practice Around Screen Scraping in the Common Law World and Its Open Banking Watershed Moment,* 30 Wash. Int'l L. J. 28, 53–54 (2020). Regarding the discussions before about these two approaches to OB, *see* Chapter 1.

42 BNP Paribas, *World Payments Report* 2018, at 23 (2018), https://world-paymentsreport.com/wp-content/uploads/sites/5/2018/10/World-Payments-Report-2018.pdf.

43 *Third Party Providers*, Open Banking, www.openbanking.org.uk/providers/third-party-providers/ (last visited Sep. 3, 2019) (hereinafter *Third Party Providers*).

44 FCA, *Payment Services and Electronic Money – Our Approach: The FCA's Role under the Payment Services Regulations 2017 and the Electronic Money*

Regulations 2011, at 6 (June 2019), www.fca.org.uk/publication/finalised-guidance/fca-approach-payment-services-electronic-money-2017.pdf

45 *About Us*, Open Banking, www.openbanking.org.uk/about-us/ (last visited July 2, 2019) (hereinafter *About OB*); CMA, *Retail Banking Market Investigation: Final Report* 441 (Aug. 9, 2016), https://assets.publishing.service.gov.uk/media/57ac9667e5274a0f6c00007a/retail-banking-market-investigation-full-final-report.pdf.

46 Rebekah Tunstead, *Open Banking Regulators Have Failed to "Pull the Banks to Order,"* Bobsguide (Dec. 13, 2018), www.bobsguide.com/guide/news/2018/Dec/13/open-banking-regulators-have-failed-to-pull-the-banks-to-order/.

47 *Id.*

48 *Open Banking March Highlights*, Open Banking (Apr. 12, 2019), www.openbanking.org.uk/about-us/latest-news/open-banking-march-highlights/ (hereinafter *Open Banking March Highlights*). The CMA9 include "Barclays plc, Lloyds Banking Group plc, Santander, Danske, HSBC, RBS, Bank of Ireland, Nationwide and AIBG." *Open Banking Publishes Version 3.1.1. of the Open Banking Standard*, Open Banking (Mar. 15, 2019), www.openbanking.org.uk/about-us/news-release-archive/open-banking-publishes-version-3-1-1-of-the-open-banking-standard/.

49 *Open Banking March Highlights*, *supra* note 48.

50 *Open Banking Limited*, Companies House (Oct. 21, 2016), https://beta.companieshouse.gov.uk/company/10440081 (last visited Oct. 3, 2019).

51 A quasi-public entity is delegated by a government agency to exercise its regulatory power and hence has a more public nature; commentators argue that this regulatory design could be an appropriate organizational model of financial regulators when implementing RegTech development policies. *See* Yang & Tsang, *supra* note 1, at 403–4.

52 *See* Chapter 4, Section 2.1.1.

53 In the UK, the separation of the Prudential Regulation Authority (the "PRA"), which focuses on financial stability and soundness concerns, and the FCA, which focuses on consumer protection and competition enhancement, aims to correct the failures of the pre-global-financial-crisis system where the Financial Service Authority (the "FSA") solely regulated financial services. *See* Elizabeth F. Brown & Edward F. Buckley, *A Preliminary Look at State Structures for Regulating Financial Services*, 87 U. Cin. L. Rev. 891, 903–4 (2019); Omar Salem & Jerome Roche, *Individual Accountability in Financial Services – the UK and US Compared*, Oxford Bus. L. Blog (Aug. 28, 2019), www.law.ox.ac.uk/BUSINESS-LAW-BLOG/BLOG/2019/08/INDIVIDUAL-ACCOUNTABILITY-FINANCIAL-SERVICES-UK-AND-US-COMPARED.

54 CMA, *Towards the CMA: CMA Guidance* 4, 8–9 (July 15, 2013), https://assets.publishing.service.gov.uk/government/uploads/system/uploads/attachment_data/file/212285/CMA1_-_Towards_the_CMA.pdf. *See also id.* at 8 (noting that "the Financial Conduct Authority . . . has a duty to promote competition but no competition powers as such.").

55 *See id.* at 9.

56 Gavin Littlejohn, Ghela Boskovich, & Richard Prior, *United Kingdom: The Butterfly Effect*, *in* Open Banking 173, 186–87 (Linda Jeng ed., Oxford University Press, 2022) (http://doi.org/10.1093/oso/9780197582879.003.0010).

57 *Id.* at 181.

58 *See id.* at 187.

59 CMA, *Annual Report on Concurrency* 27–28 (Apr. 10, 2019), https://assets. publishing.service.gov.uk/government/uploads/system/uploads/attachment_ data/file/811431/ACR_PV2406.pdf. The competition powers of the FCA are said to be less extensive as those of the CMA. Caroline Hobson, Simon Morris, Alison McHaffie, & Jacqueline Vallat, *First Use of FCA Competition Powers: Flexing Its Muscles*, Thomson Reuters (Mar. 28, 2019), https://uk.practicallaw. thomsonreuters.com/w-019-6084?transitionType=Default&contextData=%2 8sc.Default%29.

60 CMA & FCA, *Memorandum of Understanding between the Competition and Markets Authority and the Financial Conduct Authority – Concurrent Competition Powers* 7 (July 2019), www.fca.org.uk/publication/mou/fca-cma-concurrent-competition-powers-mou.pdf.

61 Directive 2015/2366, *supra* note 22, art. 4(17), at 58.

62 *See* Winn, *supra* note 16, at 26–28. In the context of the UK's Open Banking, ASP-SPs embrace "banks, building societies and payment companies." *Account Providers*, Open Banking, www.openbanking.org.uk/providers/account-providers/ (last visited Dec. 6, 2019).

63 Open Banking, *Open Banking: Guidelines for Open Data Participants* 8 (July 2018), www.openbanking.org.uk/wp-content/uploads/Guidelines-for-Open-Data-Participants.pdf (hereinafter OB Guidelines). Concerning the composition of the CMA9, *see supra* note 48 and accompanying text.

64 *See* Section 2.1.1.

65 *Id.*

66 *See* Section 2.1.3.

67 Open Banking, *Open Banking: Operational Guidelines* 19 (Apr. 30, 2019), www.openbanking.org.uk/wp-content/uploads/Operational-Guidelines-v1.1.0-master-01.05.2019.pdf.

68 *See* Section 2.1.3.

69 *See, e.g.* Simonetta Vezzoso, *Fintech, Access to Data, and the Role of Competition Policy, in* Competition and Innovation 30, 32 (V. Bagnoli ed., 2018), https://dx.doi.org/10.2139/ssrn.3106594; Directive 2015/2366, *supra* note 22, recital 39, at 41; *Third Party Providers*, *supra* note 43. Regarding the definition of these two TPPs, *see supra* note 23 and accompanying text.

70 Vezzoso, *supra* note 69, at 30.

71 Huang, *supra* note 28, at 392. In addition to FinTech startups, BigTechs may benefit from OB. Douglas Arner, Ross Buckley, Kuzi Charamba, Artem Sergeev, & Dirk Zetzsche, *BigTech and Platform Finance: Governing FinTech 4.0 for Sustainable Development* 33 (UNSW Law Research Paper No. 21–57, 2021; University of Hong Kong Faculty of Law Research Paper No. 2021/043), https:// ssrn.com/abstract=3915275; Dirk Zetzsche, William A. Birdthistle, Douglas W. Arner, & Ross P. Buckley, *Digital Finance Platforms: Toward A New Regulatory Paradigm*, 23 U. Penn. J. Bus. L. 1, 57–58 (2020).

72 *About OB*, *supra* note 45.

73 *See* Oscar Borgogno & Giuseppe Colangelo, *Consumer Inertia and Competition-Sensitive Data Governance: The Case of Open Banking* 3, 8–9, 11 (Jan. 3, 2020), https://ssrn.com/abstract=3513514.

74 PYMNTS, *PSD2's Elephant In The Room*, PYMNTS.com (Apr. 2, 2019), www.pymnts.com/bank-regulation/2019/tokenio-limited-psd2-api-standardization-user-data/.

75 Margaret Doyle, Rahul Sharma, Christopher Ross, & Vishwanath Sonnad, *Deloitte, How to Flourish in an Uncertain Future: Open Banking* 7, 9 (Deloitte UK, 2017).

76 *Id.* The whitelist is mainly provided by the Open Banking Directory that lists the participants capable of "operating in the Open Banking Ecosystem, as required by the CMA Order." *Website Glossary*, Open Banking, www.openbanking.org. uk/about-us/glossary/ (last visited Nov. 5, 2019). However, a whitelisting process for entities such as PCWs may be set up as an extra arrangement to bring them into the whitelist. Doyle et al., *supra* note 75, at 9. To be sure, the whitelisting is generally based on, for instance, whether TPPs meet high security standards because security is of vital importance to data sharing. CMA, *supra* note 45, at 458.

77 OB Guidelines, *supra* note 63, at 5.

78 *Third Party Providers*, *supra* note 43.

79 *Id.*

80 *See* OB Guidelines, *supra* note 63, at 4. "Sensitive payment data" is defined under PSD2 as the data which could be exploited to carry out fraud and includes personalized security credentials. Directive 2015/2366, *supra* note 22, art. 4(32), at 59. The PISPs "shall . . . not store sensitive payment data of the payment service user." *Id.* art. 66(3)(e), at 92. The AISPs "shall . . . not request sensitive payment data linked to the payment accounts." *Id.* art. 67(2)(e), at 93.

81 *Single Rule Book Q&A: On the Access to Names and Surnames through the API*, EBA, https://eba.europa.eu/single-rule-book-qa/-/qna/view/publicId/2018_4081 (last visited Sep. 27, 2019). To be sure, data such as log-in credentials or passwords would not be transmitted. *What is Open Banking?*, Open Banking, www.openbanking.org.uk/customers/what-is-open-banking/ (last visited Sep. 27, 2019).

82 *See* Sections 2.1.1 and 2.1.4.

83 *See* FCA, *supra* note 44, at 91–92, 179–80.

84 Directive 2015/2366, *supra* note 22, art. 95(2), at 104.

85 EBA, *Final Report: Guidelines on the Security Measures for Operational and Security Risks of Payment Services under Directive (EU) 2015/2366* (PSD2) 5, 19 (2017), https://eba.europa.eu/sites/default/documents/files/documents/ 10180/2060117/d53bf08f-990b-47ba-b36f-15c985064d47/Final%20report%20 on%20EBA%20Guidelines%20on%20the%20security%20measures% 20for%20operational%20and%20security%20risks%20under%20PSD2%20 (EBA-GL-2017-17).pdf.

86 *See* Vezzoso, *supra* note 69, at 37.

87 *See, e.g.*, *id.* at 36; Colangelo & Borgogno, *supra* note 23, at 23.

88 *See, e.g.*, Olaf van Gorp, *PSD2 & Open Banking: The Role of API Management*, Akana (Apr. 4, 2018), www.akana.com/blog/psd2-open-banking-role-api-management; Hakan Eroglu, *Comparing the Berlin Group and Open Banking UK API Standards for PSD2*, Finextra (Dec. 13, 2017), www.finextra.com/ blogposting/14834/comparing-the-berlin-group-and-open-banking-uk-api-standards-for-psd2 (noting that the EBA's RTS "for PSD2 specifies only technical framework conditions and no interface standard.").

89 *EBA Publishes Final Draft Technical Standards on Home-host Cooperation under PSD2*, EBA (July 31, 2018), https://eba.europa.eu/-/eba-publishes-final-draft-technical-standards-on-home-host-cooperation-under-psd2.

90 Doyle et al., *supra* note 75, at 8.

91 Martin Haering, *Open Banking APIs Need Standards*, Finextra (May 11, 2018), www.finextra.com/blogposting/15350/open-banking-apis-need-standards.

92 Littlejohn at al., *supra* note 56, at 189.

93 *Guidelines on Authorization and Registration under PSD2*, EBA, https://eba. europa.eu/regulation-and-policy/payment-services-and-electronic-money/ guidelines-on-authorisation-and-registration-under-psd2 (last visited Nov. 4, 2019); *Third Party Providers*, *supra* note 43. Specifically, in the UK, it is required that a TPP should register as an AISP or be authorized as a PISP. *Third Party Providers*, Open Banking, www.openbanking.org.uk/providers/third-party-providers/ (last visited Dec. 28, 2020). Even though these two types of entities are required to have professional indemnity insurance, the process to be regulated for AISPs is simpler than for PISPs. For example, PISPs should follow the minimum EUR 50,000 capital requirement, while AISPs have no capital requirements. FCA, *Payment Services and Electronic Money – Our Approach: The FCA's Role Under the Payment Services Regulations 2017 and the Electronic Money Regulations 2011*, at 25, 32 (June 2019), www.fca.org. uk/publication/finalised-guidance/fca-approach-payment-services-electronic-money-2017.pdf; *New Regulated Payment Services: Account Information Services (AIS) and Payment Initiation Services (PIS)*, FCA (Feb. 14, 2018), www. fca.org.uk/firms/new-regulated-payment-services-ais-pis (last visited Dec. 28, 2020).

94 *See* FCA, *supra* note 44, at 179.

95 *See* Peggy Valcke, Niels Vandezande, & Nathan Van de Velde, *The Evolution of Third Party Payment Providers and Cryptocurrencies under the EU's Upcoming PSD2 and AMLD4* 17–18 (SWIFT Inst. Working Paper No. 2015–001, 2015), http://ssrn.com/abstract=2665973. A high level of proportionality is introduced through, for instance, exemptions from several requirements regarding information about how to prevent negative effects in an event of termination of services, anti-money laundering ("AML") issues, and statutory auditors for AISPs. The rationale behind these exemptions is that the level of requirements should be proportionate to their specific business models. EBA, *Final Report on the EBA Guidelines under Directive (EU) 2015/2366 (PSD2) on the Information to Be Provided for the Authorisation of Payment Institutions and E-money Institutions and for the Registration of Account Information Service Providers* 8–10 (2017), https://eba.europa.eu/sites/default/documents/ files/documents/10180/1904583/f0e94433-f59b-4c24-9cec-2d6a2277b62c/ Final%20Guidelines%20on%20Authorisations%20of%20Payment%20Institu-tions%20(EBA-GL-2017-09).pdf.

96 EBA, *Consultation Paper: Draft Guidelines on the Information to be Provided for the Authorisation as Payment Institutions and E-Money Institutions and for the Registration as Account Information Service Providers* 5, 9, 78 (2016), https://eba.europa.eu/sites/default/documents/files/documents/10180/ 1646245/b8d49c1c-be4f-4b36-a5ce-e6710e00383c/Consultation Paper on draft Guidelines on authorisation and registration under PSD2 %28EBA-CP-2016-18%29.pdf.

97 *See* Chapter 4, Section 2.2.

98 Alan Brener, *EU Payment Services Regulation and International Developments*, *in* Routledge Handbook of Financial Technology and Law 159, 169 (Iris H-Y Chiu & Gudula Deipenbrock eds., 2021) (https://doi.org/10.4324/ 9780429325670).

99   *See* Pinar Ozcan & Markos Zachariadis, *Open Banking as a Catalyst for Industry Transformation: Lessons Learned from Implementing PSD2 in Europe* 3, 13 (SWIFT Institute Working Paper, July 2021), https://ssrn.com/abstract=3984857.
100 *See* Jeng, *supra* note 14, at 6; Brad Carr, *From Open Banking to Open Data and Beyond: Competition and the Future of Banking*, *in* Open Banking 303, 312–13 (Linda Jeng ed., Oxford University Press, 2022) (http://doi.org/10.1093/oso/9780197582879.001.0015).
101 Barney Reynolds, *Shearman & Sterling Discusses How UK Banking Is Affecting Global FinTech*, The CLS Blue Sky Blog (Apr. 19, 2021), https://clsbluesky.law.columbia.edu/2021/04/19/shearman-sterling-discusses-how-uk-banking-is-affecting-global-fintech/.
102 *See* Liu, *supra* note 41, at 61.
103 Borgogno & Colangelo, *supra* note 73, at 1, 11.

4   Open Banking or Open Only to Banks? A Comparative Perspective in Regulatory Policies from the EU and the UK to Taiwan

Both Chapters 2 and 3 furnished the grounds for promoting OB through regulatory intervention and appraised the EU's and the UK's experiences. In comparison with the EU and UK compulsory approach, the regulatory strategies of OB adopted by the Taiwanese government appear to differ. The Taiwanese government advances rhetoric on certain regulatory goals such as promoting data-driven innovation of the financial market through OB and ensuring competition in the modern digital economy. However, it is doubtful that Taiwan will achieve these goals via the voluntary approach to OB. Therefore, this chapter aims to examine the Taiwanese regulatory strategies as a case study to test—through a comparative lens—the lessons learned in the EU and the UK on the institutional design for FinTech regulators. In particular, we try to envision how an independent regulator should be designed to best focus its efforts on ensuring FinTech-driven innovation and competition.

Section 1 depicts the status of digital finance and the current regulatory policies in developing OB in Taiwan. Section 2 presents a comparison between the OB regulatory policies in the UK, the EU, and Taiwan. Section 3 identifies the defects in Taiwan's OB regulatory policies, parsing out, in particular, how their design might inhibit the ostensible regulatory goals to harness effects of data-driven innovation on competition in retail financial markets and, in turn, enhance consumer welfare. This section also offers explanations, beyond mere technical factors, for Taiwan's divergent regulatory system.[1] Section 4 offers a summary of the earlier discussions related to Taiwan's OB regulatory system.

1. Development of Open Banking in Taiwan

1.1 An Overview

As discussed earlier, digital transformations in modern finance center on information; more specifically, these transformations derive not only from

DOI: 10.4324/9781003126324-4

information's impact on business but also from the corresponding regulatory issues.[2] Likewise, the rise of new participants illustrates how information plays a crucial role in influencing the development of modern finance due to these new participants' informational advantages.[3]

The aforementioned phenomena—the information-driven digital transformation in modern finance—can be observed in Taiwan. Specifically, the regulatory policies on FinTech and the modern financial markets in Taiwan have been focusing on information to the extent that the regulator aims to foster financial innovation by integrating financial data.[4] Furthermore, the phenomenon in which information characterizes both modern financial markets and the corresponding regulation paves the way for the OB emphasis. Accordingly, Taiwanese financial regulators have concentrated on the openness of data since 2018.[5] Furthermore, these regulators have likewise emphasized the sharing of data between financial institutions under the same financial holding company, between unrelated financial institutions, and between nonfinancial institutions (such as TSPs) and financial institutions since late 2021.[6] One commentator noted that future challenges—such as managing the associated risks, establishing standards of sharing data, and/or regulating the data recipients—will surround the aforementioned development.[7] Nevertheless, the trend toward OB in Taiwan differs from the trend in the EU and the UK, in at least two major overarching respects as well as in certain substantive regulatory respects.[8] First of all, while new market participants emerge—thanks to technological innovation—in the Taiwanese financial markets, the markets have long been characterized as "overbanked."[9] As we will explain here, this feature to a certain degree establishes the grounds for developing OB in Taiwan by emphasizing that the introduction of FinTech companies to the markets could ultimately encourage financial innovation as the competitive landscape might change.[10] Moreover, there appears to be some obstacles on the path toward OB in Taiwan due to influence exerted by the traditional banking industry.[11] This influence seems to be the reason why the OB regulatory policies in Taiwan may have limited efficacy.

1.2 A Foreseeable Path in Taiwan: Overbanking, Open Banking, and Open Finance

As discussed before, the financial markets in Taiwan have encountered the overbanking conundrum.[12] This, of course, is one of the factors contributing to the trend toward OB reforms in Taiwan. Specifically, overbanking leads to entry barriers facing new market players such as FinTech startups because banks are not profitable enough and may not be willing to welcome new participants, thereby hindering financial inclusion.[13] Overbanking, which gives rise to intense intra-industry competition and, thus, negatively affects bank profitability,[14] would bring about several challenges that merit regulators' attention.

The first of those challenges is that excessively large banking systems may theoretically be associated with overly risky banks as such an expansive banking system creates a fiercely competitive environment where banks may engage in risker activities to seek profits. This can lead to a system that becomes "too large to save" depending on the magnitude of bank failures.[15] The second challenge is the introduction of innovative technologies to financial markets as this brings potential new entrants to the market;[16] however, in an overbanked environment, entry barriers may prevent those new potential participants from opportunities to be admitted into the market.[17]

Since technological innovation has been employed in the financial industry to allow digital finance in Taiwan to flourish, the Taiwanese financial market has witnessed the emergence of new service providers, such as the FinTech startups, in the payment sector.[18] However, while these new FinTech entrants, such as TSPs, have entered into the payment industry owing to their ability to facilitate the management of information,[19] they may confront barriers—generated by incumbent banks—against expanding their business.[20] Accordingly, the essential problems remain; FinTech startups face entry barriers, which, in turn, impacts the ability to achieve financial inclusion and, thus prohibits the promotion of innovation.[21] The benefits of enhancing financial inclusion include not only bringing more alternatives for consumers but also generally helping economic growth.[22] Accordingly, regulatory intervention seems to be favorable in this regard. While the Taiwanese market is overbanked, it would be beneficial to encourage nonbank FinTech firms to enter the markets, so as to improve the competitive structure of the retail financial markets by launching innovation into financial services.[23]

On the basis of the earlier insights, working out a suitable regulatory-design solution to the problems in an overbanked environment is of vital importance to the Taiwanese markets. As those problems are associated with the hold incumbent banks maintain over the data new entrants would use to facilitate information flow, requiring private controllers or owners of information such as banks to release information on clients' accounts to new FinTech entrants may be helpful, as illustrated by PSD2.[24] The OB policy, which is based on facilitating information flow among a variety of players in a platform-banking ecosystem,[25] is compatible with the aforementioned need to promote the provision of information.[26] Put another way, the path toward OB in Taiwan is supposed to improve competitive dynamics in retail financial markets to achieve financial inclusion. This would ultimately pave the way for open finance where consumers have a variety of options for financial services or products thanks to innovation fostered under OB policies.[27] Nonetheless, as we will explain in the following sections, the OB regulation in Taiwan is voluntary, which differs from the EU and UK mandatory model. We will then analyze whether this voluntary style of OB is truly effective.

1.3 Current State

When it comes to the trend toward OB in Taiwan, Taiwanese financial markets have debated over how to implement this trend at a public policy level. For example, ever since the issues of OB drew regulators' attention in 2018, commentators have noted that consumers' lack of trust in banks in Taiwan may be one of the obstacles to OB due to concerns related to cybersecurity and data privacy (or the service process related to when their data would be released by the banks).[28] In light of the apparent obstacles, we describe here the main characteristics of the current OB regulatory policies in Taiwan and then, assess whether they truly address the concerns mentioned earlier or, furthermore, if they raise additional concerns.[29]

To start, compared with OB as it is promoted in the EU and the UK by mandating banks to provide access to customers' accounts and associated data,[30] the OB regulatory policies in Taiwan appear to be more voluntary. That is, the Taiwanese regulators merely encourage banks to participate in OB reforms on a voluntary basis.[31] As discussed subsequently, this characteristic manifests different features of Taiwan's OB regulatory policies such as the establishment of API standards and the selection of the FinTech firms that could join OB.[32]

Next, with respect to structural policies on OB, private organizations or institutions that are not governmental organs play an important role in Taiwan. Specifically, the FSC requires the Bankers Association of the Republic of China (BAROC), a self-regulatory organization (SRO),[33] to develop the self-regulation policies for OB promotion.[34] The financial regulator, namely the FSC, serves only as the governmental body to which the BAROC submits a report, which contains their policies and relevant documentation, for record keeping purposes rather than for approval.[35] In addition, the Financial Information Service Co., Ltd. (FISC), an institution with the Ministry of Finance of Taiwan as one of its majority shareholders,[36] was required to establish the common API standards.[37] Further, the task force studying the API standards, which is under the FISC, consists of 15 representatives from different banks.[38] As shown on the left hand side of Figure 4.1 (Open Banking in Taiwan), the FISC has been acting as an institution coordinating interbank financial information; TSPs, however, can only interact with certain banks as the latter possess the control over the data.[39] Nonetheless, once the OB policies are established and enacted in Taiwan, as shown on the right-hand side of Figure 4.1, there will be an "open API management platform" operated by the FISC, which would play an intermediate role in connecting banks and TSPs (as both of them could register to provide and obtain access to data thereon when customers could leverage their own data).[40]

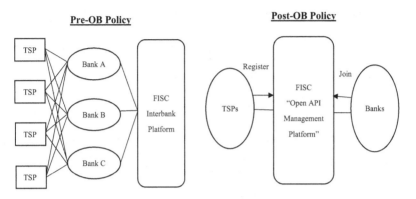

Figure 4.1 Open Banking in Taiwan.

Source: *Open API Framework*, FISC, *supra* note 38, at 15.

In addition to the OB regulatory policies, some supportive strategies are being developed in Taiwan. For instance, as interoperability is crucial in facilitating information flow for the FinTech market,[41] Taiwan adopted the Open API Specification (OAS).[42] The OAS is established by the OpenAPI Initiative (OAI), which is an open-source and technical community under the Linux Foundation.[43]

Lastly, Taiwan adopted a means of opening different types of data in a phased fashion. Specifically, as shown in Table 4.1 (Timeline of the Three Phases of the Open Banking in Taiwan), the search for public data could be realized in phase one, indicating that public information regarding banks' services and products could be accessed and aggregated.[44] This was expected to be achieved by the end of September 2019;[45] however, phase one was actually completed in October 2019.[46] In phase two, it was expected that customers' account data could be accessed and integrated with customers' consent by the end of December 2019.[47] However, in August 2020, it was reported that there was an obstacle to this phase due to the banks' unwillingness to truly open their data pool and their fear of liabilities in the case of data leakage.[48] Nevertheless, it was reported in November 2020 that phase two had finally commenced.[49] It was also reported in December 2020 that several TSPs and banks cooperatively participated in this phase.[50] As reported in April 2021, the customers' account data has been opened up, and the corresponding services on the basis of the opened data in phase two have been proffered.[51] Ultimately, customers' transaction information was initially expected to be released in phase three so as to carry on transactions online in the second quarter of the year 2020.[52] Nonetheless, as of this writing, this phase has not been completed yet; it was reported in both July and October 2021 that the progress of this phase was delayed.[53]

Table 4.1 Timeline of the Three Phases of Open Banking in Taiwan.

	Type of Data to Be Opened	*Expected Timeline and Status*
Phase 1	Public information regarding banks' services and products	Expected to be completed by the end of September 2019; services have been rendered since October 2019
Phase 2	Customers' account data; based on customers' consent	Initially expected to be completed by December 2019; actually commenced in November 2020; services have been provided since April 2021
Phase 3	Customers' transaction information	Expected to be completed in the second quarter of 2020; not yet completed as of this writing; progress was delayed

Source: the Authors

2. Comparing the Different Approaches to Open Banking in the UK, the EU, and Taiwan

2.1 Seven Features of Open Banking Regulatory Policies in Taiwan

2.1.1 Voluntary Approach Implemented and Led by Banks

As discussed before, both the UK and EU regulations require ASPSPs (e.g., banks) to provide access to data, and regulators have a significant influence in leading such a compulsory approach.[54] In contrast, Taiwan has adopted a voluntary approach.[55] One reason Taiwan adopted this approach is that the FSC expected that OB would be more easily promoted in Taiwan without amending laws, since legal amendments would incur costs and be time-consuming.[56] As such, the FSC relies on a private industry association, that is, the BAROC, to draft self-regulations so as to promote OB in Taiwan.[57] This approach appears to follow the historic regulatory trajectory of the FSC when trying to foster financial competition and innovation. As explained here, this trajectory invites critics due to the potential influence from the banking industry.[58]

2.1.2 *Participation of Parties Who Would Open Data on a Voluntary Basis*

When it comes to the regulated parties who should provide access to their data pool, these parties mandated under both the PSD2 and the UK's OB initiative are ASPSPs, which include mainly banks.[59] In Taiwan, the entities that would open their data are also banks;[60] their participation in OB initiatives is, however, on a voluntary basis.[61] As such, if any issues that might harm consumers arise, such as the case of data leakage, the FSC suggested that banks may need to bear the liabilities.[62] This treatment of banks under the voluntary approach might un-incentivize them to join OB or offer some ostensible reason why they cannot or will not join. As mentioned before, we have observed such a phenomenon in the second phase of promoting OB in Taiwan.[63]

The intersection of OB and digital-only banking should merit Taiwanese regulators' attention.[64] It is noteworthy that combining these new business models into a novel platform business model of banking—that is, banking-as-a-platform (BaaP)—would generate a higher degree of openness.[65] For instance, Fidor Bank AG (Fidor), an innovative German digital-only bank adopting an OB approach, thereby realized the concept of BaaP with its "API-based microservice architecture."[66] Yet, such a heightened degree of financial inclusion based on the combination of OB and digital-only banks relies on promotion by a truly effective legal regime. Therefore, although OB and digital-only banks are only now developing and Taiwan's relevant policies have yet to be settled, a greater digital financial inclusion would be achieved in Taiwan by the aid of truly effective regulatory policies.[67]

2.1.3 *Parties Accessing Data Appear Diverse But Are Hand-Picked by Banks*

Although the UK, the EU, and Taiwan primarily grant data access to payment services providers, those parties with data access in Taiwan are less clearly defined. According to the official comment on the Draft of the Self-Regulation Governing OB in Taiwan, these providers may include but are not limited to (1) electronic payment institutions,[68] (2) electronic stored value card issuers,[69] (3) online platforms, and (4) software services providers.[70] Such a scope seems quite wide and diverse.

Notwithstanding the possibility that many FinTech firms in Taiwan might have access to data pools because, as mentioned, of the wide scope, it may not be the case in practice. According to the aforementioned self-regulation formulated by the BAROC, it is not the FSC that may decide on the TSPs that can be the beneficiaries of OB. Rather, these TSPs are assessed, selected, and even governed by the banks alone.[71] As further discussed subsequently, this may demonstrate how the FSC has been historically influenced by incumbent financial institutions like the banking industry when developing FinTech-related policies.[72]

2.1.4 Step-by-Step Approach to Opening Data Up: Potential Legal Issues Regarding Scope of Data to Be Opened Remain

In regard to the scope of data to be opened, the Taiwanese government adopts a step-by-step approach to opening up different types of data in three phases.[73] The scope of data opened in phases two and three in Taiwan are similar to the scope of data opened in the UK and the EU. Nevertheless, nontransactional data, which was first opened in October 2019, seems to be associated less with the real goal of fostering financial innovation.[74] Thus, opening the data types reserved for phases two and three will be more meaningful to accomplishment of true OB. However, since OB is a comparatively new concept in Taiwan, legal issues regarding the scope of opened data will arise.[75] For example, some argue that the issues may ultimately be related more to consumer empowerment to exploit their data.[76] Accordingly, legal issues such as consumers' privacy should be carefully addressed by clearly defining the scope of data to be opened.[77]

2.1.5 Timeline and Scope of Opening Data Are Subject to the Participation of Banks

When it comes to the question of who determines the scope of data to be opened, there are also differences between the UK and EU approaches and Taiwan's. Specifically, the details, including the scope or type of data that should be excluded, are determined in corresponding regulations and rules in the UK and the EU.[78] By contrast, even though the FSC announced a step-by-step approach to opening different types of data in Taiwan, the actual realization of this timeline seems to be subject to the participation of banks. For instance, as mentioned before, the promotion of OB experienced some difficulty in phase two as banks were not willing to join, rendering the promotion of OB challenging.[79]

2.1.6 The Banking Industry Establishes API Standards

In regard to the API standards, the approaches adopted by the UK, the EU, and Taiwan differ as well. In comparison with both the UK and EU approaches, which involve regulators and other third parties, rather than only banks, the creation of common API standards in Taiwan is controlled mainly by banks. This measure, together with the voluntary approach to OB in general, may be flexible; however, the UK's common API standards under its compulsory approach are deemed to lead to lower administrative costs.[80] In Taiwan, a task force was established under an "Open API Committee" in order to look into the API standards.[81] Both the task force and the aforementioned committee are under the FISC and composed of banks or other traditional financial institutions.[82] TSPs play a trivial role in the creation of common API standards in that their opinions are collected by a university instead of participating directly in the aforementioned committee; the FISC performs its part in coordinating between the university collecting TSPs' opinions and the aforementioned committee.[83] A commentator argued that with the FISC's involvement, the regulatory design seems to be a mixture of a mode in which the government merely encourages OB by listing the API types from which banks could choose and of a mode adopted by the EU and the UK where a coordinating entity such as OBIE is involved.[84] However, under this mode in which the FISC coordinates between banks and TSPs, together with the feature that banks governs TSPs (which will be discussed in Section 2.1.7), it was pointed out that ensuring that TSPs' opinions could be heard is critical.[85] In addition, under Taiwan's phased approach, the issues regarding information security are significant at phase two, where consumers' information is involved; thus, establishing proper API standards is critical. Nevertheless, the inclusion of TSPs during phase two also matters; otherwise, the value of OB could not be truly realized.[86]

In addition, when considering not only the composition but also the actual functioning of the committee, we observe that the role of FinTech startups seems—in a sense—to be ignored. Specifically, even though a group of external consultants are involved in the rule-making process, their role is limited and not significant enough to offer genuine assistance to the FinTech startups.[87] According to a commentator who led an industry association composed of FinTech firms in Taiwan, TSPs had no opportunity to participate in the process of setting common API and security standards, which are associated with the data to be opened in Taiwan's OB phases.[88]

2.1.7   Third-Party Service Providers Are Assessed, Selected, and Governed by Banks

Since the banking industry, in practice, is authorized to promote OB policies in Taiwan, access to data by TSPs is largely subject to banks' decisions. Specifically, banks are entitled to assess qualifications of TSPs, such as their operation, experience, expertise, and risk management with respect to information or cyber security, before making decisions to select the providers with which banks would cooperate.[89] This might be the case because banks, rather than TSPs, are held responsible for any disputes in the first place.[90]

However, as discussed before, the scope of the TSPs that may be eligible to join OB would be broad in form alone.[91] Banks, in substance, control the entry to OB via the aforementioned processes of assessment and selection.[92] Further, the TSPs that enroll in OB must fulfill banks' or competent regulators' requirements to provide related data (including transaction data) or be examined with respect to their business including, but not limited to, cyber or information security to be audited.[93] Accordingly, it appears that the TSPs are to a large extent subject to the banks' governance. If the criteria banks use to select TSPs as well as the governance measures are too strict, TSPs would face many obstacles in joining OB.[94] These policies differ from those in the UK and the EU in that competent regulators therein are the main authority governing TPPs and regulators do not rely on incumbent financial institutions (i.e., banks) to set, implement, and/or enforce standards for OB reforms.[95] In addition, as discussed before,[96] AISPs and PISPs are subject to proportionate rules in the EU's and UK's OB regulations, thereby enhancing equal opportunities for competition and bringing more TPPs into OB.[97] Now that such lenient and proportionate rules seem to be lacking in Taiwan's OB, it is doubtful that its OB reforms will be more inclusive to Taiwanese TSPs.

2.2   Comparing Open Banking Regulatory Policies in the UK, the EU, and Taiwan

The following Table 4.2 summarizes the regulatory policies promoting OB in the UK, the EU, and Taiwan discussed, thus far, in this book.

3.   Potential Pitfalls in Regulatory Policies Promoting Open Banking in Taiwan

3.1   Historical Failures of Regulatory Policies for Governing Modern Finance in Taiwan

As discussed earlier, information is relevant not only to the emergence of new market players (given their ability to facilitate information flow) but

Table 4.2 Comparison of the Regulatory Policies of OB in the UK, the EU, and Taiwan.

	UK	EU	Taiwan
Compulsory or voluntary? Who should open the data? Who may access the data?	• Compulsory • ASPSPs • PISPs & AISPs • A broad range of entities may be eligible through the process of "whitelisting."	• Compulsory • ASPSPs • PISPs & AISPs	• Voluntary • Traditional banks • TSPs • A broad range of entities may be eligible.
What is the scope of the data to be opened?	• Account information[98]	• Account information	• Phase 1: product information • Phase 2: customers' account information • Phase 3: transaction information • The timeline and scope are decided in a phased manner but subject to the participation of banks.
Who may decide the scope of the data to be opened?	• Exclusions of data to be opened largely depend on the FCA.	• Assessment of the mechanisms protecting sensitive data should be provided to competent authorities in member states	
Who may decide on the API standards?	• Co-determination by both CMA9 and "representatives of third parties and members representing the interests of consumers and SMEs."	• No mandate for the establishment of common API standards. • EBA drafted RTS.	• A task force under the FISC, which is composed of the representatives of banks or other traditional financial institutions, is in charge.

(Continued)

Table 4.2 (Continued)

	UK	EU	Taiwan
	• Open Banking Standard is adopted.		• External consultants are also involved in the rule-making process, but TSPs did not have any chance to participate in the process of setting common API standards and security standards.[99] • The OAS is adopted.
How to govern or supervise third-party providers?	• PISPs should be authorized and AISPs should be registered. • They are regulated by the FCA, providing more leniency or additional proportionality for AISPs and PISPs.	• PISPs should be authorized and AISPs should be registered. • They are regulated by competent authorities in member states, providing more leniency or additional proportionality for AISPs and PISPs.	• TSPs are assessed, selected and governed by banks alone. • No proportionate rules for TSPs.

Source: the Authors

also to the introduction of regulatory efforts to promote financial innovation.[100] In the context of OB, the regulatory response for data-driven finance aims to remove the entry barriers facing new market players by leveraging customer control over their own bank data.[101] Theoretically, with the aid of OB regulations that improve access to data, new FinTech providers could overcome entry barriers.[102] Nevertheless, the OB reforms in Taiwan differ from the approaches adopted in the UK and the EU with respect to seven distinct features we have examined.[103] Before delving into the specific pitfalls of Taiwan's OB regulation, we will demonstrate the general failures in regulatory policies—intended to promote financial innovation—that have historically been adopted in Taiwan.

In Taiwan, these regulatory policies have been critiqued for failing to achieve public interest goals of financial innovation, inclusion, and competition.[104] Specifically, Taiwan's recent regulatory reforms, which were supposed to encourage FinTech innovation, seem to be trapped in the regulator's stubborn dependence on a particular path (i.e., the regulator's persistent reliance on conventional institutional philosophy), thereby failing to meet those aforementioned public interest goals.[105] For instance, the promotion of financial innovation is the main regulatory objective of the Financial Technology Development and Innovative Experimentation Act (the FinTech Sandbox Act).[106] Nevertheless, the legislative and regulatory trajectory of the FinTech Sandbox Act demonstrates how the incumbent financial industry's influence weakens the chances that FinTech-startups-based peer-to-peer lending platforms (P2P lending platforms) will benefit from it.[107] Further, owing to the FSC's encouragement of collaboration between traditional banks and P2P lending platforms, these platforms are expected to comply with the extant regulations applied to banks.[108] Thus, it is suspected that innovation would be promoted efficaciously through the regulatory reforms illustrated earlier. Such an emphasis on collaboration between traditional financial institutions and FinTech companies is seen not only as mentioned earlier but also with regard to opening online insurance companies. Specifically, one of the latest developments of FinTech regulation in Taiwan is that insurance services can be offered online; however, the insurance entities eligible for offering such services are limited to those that are established by both a traditional financial institution and a FinTech company.[109]

Similarly, we observe that Taiwanese OB policies appear to be on a similar historical regulatory trajectory that has not been friendly to FinTech startups.[110] As discussed in further detail in Section 3.3, the FSC's emphasis on collaboration with incumbent financial institutions has led to its reliance on them in related regulatory endeavors. Potential failures of these policies were likely predictable due to the Taiwanese financial regulator's tendency toward over-conservativeness and regulatory inertia. This regulatory persistence can be explained from the perspective of regulatory capture.[111] The explanations are further supported in the following sections.

3.2 Regulatory Conservativeness Exemplified by Open Banking Reforms in Taiwan

When it comes to the regulator's conservativeness, the FSC, which is the sole financial regulator in Taiwan, arguably intends to be averse to risks and follow its previous experience when reacting to FinTech emergence.[112] This phenomenon illustrates limited effectiveness of FinTech regulation in Taiwan because the FSC might, in practice, be conservative and unwilling to change its regulatory posture.[113] A tendency toward conservativeness can be exemplified by not only the implementation of the FinTech Sandbox Act[114] but also the OB reforms in Taiwan led by the FSC's reactive attitude.[115] To dive deeper into the conservative nature of Taiwanese OB policies we begin by examining how the polices were made.

While Asia has been regarded as one of the most innovative areas when it comes to FinTech and the payment technology, OB regulatory reforms across different Asian jurisdictions differ.[116] For instance, even though the Chinese payment market has been flourishing—owing to domination by BigTechs such as Alibaba or Ant Financial therein, China is considered relatively reactive or conservative in terms of developing OB due to its wait-and-see approach.[117] In contrast, Singapore is deemed a pioneer as its financial regulator, the Monetary Authority of Singapore (the MAS), published the API Playbook in collaboration with the Association of Banks in Singapore (the ABS) in November 2016. This comprehensive playbook established guidelines for encouraging and implementing OB.[118] OB is promoted in Singapore through the guidelines but without legislation.[119] In addition, Hong Kong, another financial center in Asia and a competitor of Singapore, also started promoting OB based on the "Open API Framework for the Hong Kong Banking Sector," published by the Hong Kong Monetary Authority (the HKMA) in July 2018.[120]

Regardless of the Taiwanese FinTech startups' on-going struggle to enter the financial market,[121] Taiwan, which is not a pioneer in Asia in terms of promoting OB, considered following the voluntary approaches to OB policies adopted by Singapore and Hong Kong in October 2018.[122] Specifically, the FSC appears to be reactive and to adopt the policies similar to those in Singapore and Hong Kong when it comes to promoting OB. Therefore, in Taiwan, the supply-side push of OB, which is somehow driven by the FSC albeit with a position to let banks themselves decide on whether and how to implement OB voluntarily, seems to be more reactive.[123]

In comparison, countries such as the UK are regarded as proactive because their regulators actively initiate policies in response to the customers' needs and their demand-side payments institutions' uptake of OB initiatives. As a result, these countries become pioneers in FinTech-enabled banking and payments.[124]

Despite the regulator's reactive supply-side push in Taiwan, we cannot ignore the demand-side pull of the OB regulation, which is driven by customers and enthusiastic payments industry stakeholders including BigTechs and FinTech startups. This may be owing to their expectation that some regulatory reforms would help them overcome entry barriers.[125] For example, FinTech firms in Taiwan have expressed their willingness to be directly and explicitly regulated under specific laws and regulations in order to enter the markets in the belief that they would be trusted by potential customers.[126] Nevertheless, when making an appraisal of Taiwan's OB regulatory policies, it is found that FinTech firms do not appear to be directly regulated by public authorities. Rather, they are governed by banks based on the granted power to coordinate between banks and FinTech startups. This situation underscores that "being regulated" generates a reputational value to FinTech firms in Taiwan. Specifically, while incentives of meaningful value could theoretically refer to "symbolic rewards" that enhance regulatees' reputations,[127] "being regulated" in the case of FinTech in Taiwan seems to be deemed as a way to achieve such symbolic awards. By contrast, banks in Taiwan may be interested in OB regulation merely because they regard newly emerging FinTech firms as competitors and want to exclude them from the markets.[128] While it was argued that the battles between different stakeholders or interest groups who are interested in regulation and demand it are often seen,[129] banks in Taiwan could win such interest group competition of OB regulation. Accordingly, the FSC's approach that relies on banks—entities that may be un-incentivized to open data pools they control—should be reconsidered.

In this regard, regulators in Taiwan appear to be more conservative and make less forward-looking efforts in regulatory initiatives.[130] In other words, their reactive posture may, in part, be attributed to regulatory inertia.

3.3 Regulatory Inertia Inhabits Taiwanese Open Banking Reforms Due to Reliance on Banking Industry

This regulatory inertia is illustrated by the fact that the FSC's regulatory policies have historically relied on the banking industry—a pattern that has invited criticisms.[131] As discussed, the BAROC leads OB reforms in Taiwan by enacting self-regulatory rules.[132] The timeline and scope of data to be opened up are, to a substantial degree, subject to banks' participation.[133]

Moreover, the internal Open API Committee under the FISC, which determines the API standards, is composed solely of banks or incumbent financial institutions while external consultants mentioned in the self-regulatory rules play only a marginal role by merely providing opinions.[134] More importantly, banks have the final say through their assessment and selection of the TSPs with which they would like to cooperate.[135] The FSC's reliance on banks for financial regulation may be to blame for these circumstances. For example, in 2018, when considering whether to adopt a voluntary or mandatory approach to OB, given concerns about banks' backlash, the FSC, who had encouraged bank-FinTech partnerships, decided that the voluntary-based self-regulatory model should be implemented by banks.[136] To be in keeping with the FSC's banks-centered financial regulatory philosophy, whenever a consumer dispute arises in the context of OB, bank—rather than TSPs—should be responsible for resolving the dispute.[137]

In contrast, TPPs that may access data are defined clearly in the UK and EU OB regulations.[138] There, TPPs are subject to scaled regulation where either the authorization or the registration requirement is implemented according to the TPP type. By improving their competition conditions, such measures are expected to entice more TPPs into OB.[139] In Taiwan, though the scope of the TSPs who can access data appears to be broad according to current regulatory policy,[140] they are still subject to banks' arbitrary assessment and selection.[141] Thus, the regulatory flexibility for different types of the TSPs—based on varying terms of, for example, minimum capital requirements and competent authorities—gives the mere illusion fulfilling a broad scope.[142] As discussed subsequently, although OB, at a formal level, has been admirably promoted in Taiwan, its implementation, at a functional or substantive level, demonstrates the system's influence by and reliance on the banking industry, which has historically been observed in the FSC's regulatory policies toward FinTech development.

As a matter of legal policies, however, the dependence on the banking industry for OB implementation may help prop up the conservative posture that opens the FinTech door only to banks, leading to an increase of FinTech business that are backed by banks themselves. Therefore, such a policy may be less likely to reach the initial goal of promoting consumer financial innovation, competition, and inclusion by opening the data or APIs to FinTech startups.[143] A similar problem also arises in the OB policies in Hong Kong on which Taiwanese "voluntary-based" OB reforms are modeled.[144] In Hong Kong, it seems that the issue of how to encourage banks to join OB is critical, especially at an early phase under its voluntary approach as the regulator in Hong Kong investigated "how to nudge the banks to open up account data and enable the initiation of transactions by third parties as well."[145]

According to Karen Yu, a former Taiwanese legislator specializing in FinTech development, the FSC has been acting in favor of the banking industry as reflected in the fact that the review committee for entrance into the FinTech sandbox, half of which is composed all of government officials, often works to the advantage of the banks.[146] It is likewise not surprising that the FSC—a government agency that relies on banks for implementing and leading OB reforms—repeatedly dispenses favors to the banking industry.

While the objectives of the OB reforms are to enhance consumer financial innovation and promote competition and inclusion by eliminating the entry barriers faced by FinTech startups, it is doubtful that the voluntary-based OB reforms in Taiwan can achieve these goals. This skepticism is due to the aforementioned regulatory inertia, conservativeness of the FSC, and the prevailing private interests that might influence the FSC, at least in theory, as discussed subsequently.

3.4 Influence of Private Interests Might Spur the Regulatory Pitfalls of Open Banking in Taiwan

The regulatory pitfalls, as exemplified earlier, could be explained from the perspective of regulatory capture.[147] Specifically, the FSC has been assigned diversified missions, including to ensure financial stability and consumer protection as well as to promote financial competition, innovation, and inclusion; such diversification creates mission conflicts and regulatory dilemmas.[148] Conflicting responsibilities may theoretically cause an increasing problem that short-term concerns may override long-term goals due to industry pressure.[149] In Taiwan, the short-term concerns are the FSC's long-standing mission of maintaining financial stability (to ensure banks' short-term survival) and consumer protection, which are easier to manage by being persistently conservative,[150] while the long-term public-interest goals to promote consumer financial competition, innovation, and inclusion by changing its mindset, are harder to accomplish.[151]

In theory, regulators tend to prioritize their missions, and, consequently, industry pressures compete with each other to influence this prioritization.[152] In terms of developing FinTech, existing financial industries may have exerted undue influence on relevant regulations and policies.[153] Specifically, the FSC may have been influenced by the incumbent banks in Taiwan when it comes to developing FinTech because, with the emergence of FinTech, startups were perceived as competitors against those incumbent banks.[154] Therefore, according to a former Taiwanese legislator specializing in FinTech issues, the FSC has in reality focused on how to protect traditional banks from losing profits in FinTech, rather than on (1) how to truly achieve consumer financial inclusion, (2) how to create a level "playing field" for startups to compete, and (3) how to truly promote the innovation brought by FinTech startups.[155] In Taiwan, one way the banking industry wields such influence on the regulator is illustrated by the long-standing phenomenon of incumbent banks hiring retired governmental officials.[156] In the context of OB, the FISC, which helps implement OB in Taiwan by setting rules regarding the scope of data to be opened and API standards,[157] has governmental majority shareholders (that decide on its governance, composition, and budget) and is hence similar to the OBIE in the UK. However, the governmental bodies in Taiwan are still influenced by the banking industry to some extent. Thus, it is doubtful that OB policies in Taiwan can achieve consumer financial innovation, competition, and inclusion effectively.

The fact that private interests rather than public interests are fulfilled through regulations is reflected by not merely the OB reforms in Taiwan but also the long-standing entry barriers facing FinTech startups because policies fail to provide them access to information as further shown below.[158] As discussed, in modern finance where information, or rather data, plays a crucial role, the incumbent industry could exploit their entrenched market power at the expense of potential competitors such as FinTech startups by limiting access to information.[159] For example, the Joint Credit Information Center (the JCIC) in Taiwan, as "both a public and a private agency, with NGO (Non-governmental Organization) and NPO (Non-profit Organization) features," was created under an information-centered regulatory policy that aims to collect, process, and exchange credit data across all financial institutions and customers to facilitate transactions.[160] Nevertheless, its establishment and operation did not favor FinTech startups because only traditional financial institutions were granted access to its data pool.[161] Such entry barriers seem to result from the fact that the banking industry has significant influence on the JCIC and that the information stored by the JCIC is available only for the incumbent financial institutions.[162] The argument here is supported by a former legislator in Taiwan, stating the following:

> [T]he fair competition is not considered. The reason why I would say that is that, for instance, the access to JCIC data is limited to only financial intuitions but FinTech firms. If banks could meet people's financial demands in the era of digital economy, FinTech is not necessary. Thus, when we discuss fair competition regarding regulation, should we also examine whether the fair competition exist across the financial services market? Otherwise, it is not a fair market. To a government, we should do our best to maintain a market with fair competition.[163]

Notwithstanding that the JCIC operation might have not been in favor of FinTech companies, it was reported in November 2020 that the JCIC might establish a separate data pool to release data to FinTech companies by the end of 2021.[164] It is indeed an improvement; however, it also mirrors the reality that FinTech companies have long been facing difficulties in this regard. Accordingly, the actual operation of the data pool, which FinTech companies were granted access to, is worth studying in the future. By combining the aforementioned theoretical implications with the commentators' practical opinions from the perspective of financial markets competition and FinTech development, we will thus propose policy solutions in the next chapter.

4. Conclusion

This chapter examined the OB regulatory policies in Taiwan and compared them with the counterparts in the EU and the UK. In comparison with the compulsory approach adopted in the EU and the UK, OB has been promoted through the self-regulatory rules developed by the BAROC. The BAROC also controls the FinTech startups' entry to OB by assessing and choosing the FinTech startups to which banks would open their data pools up. We discussed possible pitfalls for this approach as banks and FinTech startups are sometimes competitors, and, as such, banks have no incentives to open data pools up and truly promote OB. In order to address the aforementioned issues, we will propose a solution in Chapter 5. This solution is based on organizational design of financial regulators. In general, the findings in this chapter reveal the potential difficulties in unleashing the benefits of FinTech while simultaneously mitigating market failures from a public policy perspective. These difficulties, in particular, seem to stem from an inappropriate organizational design of financial regulators in the era of FinTech. We will further elaborate on this notion in the next chapter.

Notes

1 For instance, at a theoretical level, lack of expertise is one of the technical reasons for the regulatory defects. It results in information inadequacy and a failure to foresee consequences of regulation. Anthony I. Ogus, *Regulation: Legal Form and Economic Theory* 56 (Hart Publishing, 2004) (http://dx.doi.org/10.5040/9781472559647).
2 *See* Chapter 2, Section 2.
3 *See* Chapter 2, Section 2.1.
4 For example, in Taiwan, the Financial Supervisory Commission (the "FSC"), the sole watchdog in Taiwanese financial markets, established "FinTechSpace"

in 2018 in order to foster financial innovation by providing different services in a physical place where the industry, regulators, and academia are brought together. In particular, the "Digital Sandbox," which is one of the services offered as the first FinTech open API common platform, aims to create an environment where financial innovation could be tested on the basis of the digital data resources from a wide range of FinTech-related API suppliers to be integrated in this Digital Sandbox program, building "a bridge between incumbents and startups to increase more collaboration opportunities." *Digital Sandbox: About Digital Sandbox*, FinTechSpace, www.fintechspace.com.tw/space_resource/digital-sandbox/?lang=en (last visited Apr. 5, 2020). It demonstrates that information is crucial for both developing and regulating modern finance since an environment beneficial for developing financial innovation is based on the integrated financial data.

5 *See* Zhen-Ling Peng (彭禎伶), *Jin Guan Hui: Jin Nian Yan Yi "Kai Fang Yin Hang" Tui Dong Jia Gou* (金管會：今年研議「開放銀行」推動架構) [*The FSC: The Framework for Promoting Open Banking Will Be Developed This Year*], Gong Shang Shi Bao (工商時報) [Commercial Times], (Mar. 13, 2018), https://ctee.com.tw/news/finance/102117.html.

6 Cheng-Yun Tsang (臧正運), *Yin Hang Ye Zi Liao Zhi Li De Fa Zhi Tiao Zhan* (銀行業資料治理的法制挑戰) [*The Legal Challenges of Data Governance in the Banking Industry*], 9 Tai Wan Fa Lu Ren (台灣法律人) [Formosan Jurist] 70, 73 (2022).

7 *See id.* at 74–76.

8 The comparison of the content between these OB regulations will be drawn later. *See* Section 2.

9 The then FSC Chairman, Wellington L. Koo, pointed out that the banking sector in Taiwan was characterized by overbanking due to the high density of bank branches in Taiwan. Gong Shang Shi Bao (工商時報), *Gong Shang She Lun: Overbanking Yu Kai Fang Chun Wang Yin Lun Bian* (工商社論》Overbanking與開放純網銀論辯) [*Gong Shang Editorial: Debate over Overbanking and Opening Up Digital-Only Banks*], Zhong Shi Xin Wen Wang (中時新聞網) [China Times], (Apr. 22, 2019), www.chinatimes.com/newspapers/20190422000188-260202?chdtv. At that time, there were 6,247 bank branches in Taiwan. Zhen-Ling Peng (彭禎伶) & Qiao-Yi Wei (魏喬怡), *Chun Wang Yin Neng Zhong Jie Overbanking?* (純網銀能終結Overbanking?) [*Can Digital-Only Banks Terminate Overbanking?*], Yahoo! Xin Wen (雅虎新聞) [Yahoo! News], (Mar. 12, 2019), https://tw.news.yahoo.com/%E7%B4%94%E7%B6%B2%E9%8A%80%E8%83%BD%E7%B5%82%E7%B5%90overbanking-215005123-finance.html. In addition, as of the end of 2018, there were 19,222,440 adults in Taiwan. *Administrative Announcement* (行政公告), Ministry of the Interior (內政部) (Jan. 4, 2019), www.moi.gov.tw/chi/chi_news/news_detail.aspx?src=news&sn=15355&type_code=01. Therefore, if we calculate bank branch density per 100,000 adults in Taiwan, it was approximately 32.5 bank branches. According to the data from the World Bank, however, the 2018 global median in aggregate is approximately 12.7 bank branches; among the reporting countries listed in the data provided by the World Bank, Taiwan would be ranked approximately 21st. *See Commercial bank branches (per 100,000 adults)*, The World Bank, https://data.worldbank.org/indicator/FB.CBK.BRCH.P5?end=2018&locations=1W&most_recent_value_desc=true&start=2012&view=chart (last visited Dec. 4, 2019). For a detailed description

of the Taiwanese banking system and its evolution toward an overly crowded problem, *see* Nicholas Borst & Cindy Li, Fed. Res. Bank of S.F., *Taiwan's Banking Sector Reforms: Retrospective and Outlook* 1–6 (2016). *See also id.* at 6 (noting that "[a]s a result of overcrowding, Taiwanese banks have among the lowest returns on assets and net interest margins," compared with other major Asian economies including China, Malaysia, Hong Kong, South Korea, Japan, and Singapore in 2015.).

10 *See* Section 1.2.

11 *See* Section 3.

12 *See supra* note 9 and accompanying text.

13 Cheng-Yun Tsang (臧正運), *Jin Rong Ke Ji Chuang Xin Yu Jian Li De Ping Heng* (金融科技創新與監理的平衡) [*A Balance between Financial Technology Innovation and Supervision*], Ha Fo Shang Ye Ping Lun (哈佛商業評論) [Harvard Business Review], (Jan. 1, 2017), www.hbrtaiwan.com/article_content_AR0003845.html. This cited source is the traditional Chinese edition of Harvard Business Review published in Taiwan.

14 Int'l Monetary Fund, *Global Financial Stability Report: Getting the Policy Mix Right* 32 (International Monetary Fund, 2017)

15 *See* Allen N. Berger, Leora F. Klapper, & Rima Turk-Ariss, *Bank Competition and Financial Stability*, 35 J. Fin. Serv. Res. 99, 100 (2009); ESRB, *Reports of the Advisory Scientific Committee: Is Europe Overbanked?* 10 (June 2014); *Too Much of a Good Thing? The Need for Consolidation in the European Banking Sector*, Eur. Cent. Bank (Sep. 27, 2017), www.bankingsupervision.europa.eu/press/speeches/date/2017/html/ssm.sp170927.en.html.

16 *See* Dirk A. Zetzsche, Ross P. Buckley, Douglas W. Arner, & Janos N. Barberis, *From Fintech to Techfin: The Regulatory Challenges of Data-Driven Finance*, 14 N.Y.U. J. L. & Bus. 393, 401–2 (2018); Tom C. W. Lin, *The New Financial Industry*, 65 Ala. L. Rev. 567, 576 (2014).

17 *See* Fernando Restoy, *Bank for Int'l Settlement, The European Banking Union: What Are the Missing Pieces?* 6 (2018), www.bis.org/speeches/sp181018a.pdf.

18 For how regulations, like the PSD2, can push banks to disclose information on their client's accounts to new Fintech entrants, *see* Giorgio Barba Navaretti, Giacomo Calzolari, & Alberto Franco Pozzolo, *FinTech and Banks: Friends or Foes? in* FinTech and Banking. Friends or Foes? 9, 19 (Giorgio Barba, Giacomo Calzolari, & Alberto Franco Pozzolo eds., Europeye srl, 2017), http://european-economy.eu/wp-content/uploads/2018/01/EE_2.2017-2.pdf.

19 For instance, Moneybook (a FinTech startup participating in the payment sector as a TSP) aims to provide online services that help clients manage their personal finances by, for example, linking all an individual's bank accounts with the mobile device application of Moneybook. Conceptually speaking, this type of financial service providers would facilitate the management of personal financial information. *See* Jing-Yuan Gao (高敬原), *Yi Jian Deng Ru Suo You Jin Rong Fu Wu Kai Fang Yin Hang Neng Bang Ni Sheng He Bao? FinTech Ye Zhe Xian Shen Shuo* (一鍵登入所有金融服務，開放銀行能幫你省荷包？FinTech業者現身說) [*One Click to Log-in to All the Financial Services: Can Open Banking Help You Save Money? FinTech Firms Explain*], Shu Wei Shi Dai (數位時代) [Business Next], (July 19, 2019), www.bnext.com.tw/article/54062/taiwan-open-banking-tsp-moneybook. Moneybook exemplifies the AISP in Taiwan. Hui-Xuan Li (李蕙璇), *Jie Shen Mi She Tuan 1 Tian Shi Tou Zi Ren Za Qian Bu Pa Si Pei Pao Shang Bai Xin Chuang Tuan Dui* (揭神秘社團1 天使投資人砸錢不怕

死 陪跑上百新創團隊) [*Unveiling a Mysterious Group: Angel Investors Are Not Afraid of Spending Money, Supporting Over One Hundred Startups.*], Yahoo Xin Wen (Yahoo新聞) [Yahoo News], (Oct. 14, 2019), https://tw.news. yahoo.com/%E6%8F%AD%E7%A5%9E%E7%A7%98%E7%A4%BE%E5% 9C%981-%E5%A4%A9%E4%BD%BF%E6%8A%95%E8%B3%87%E4%B A%BA%E7%A0%B8%E9%8C%A2%E4%B8%8D%E6%80%95%E6%AD% BB-%E9%99%AA%E8%B7%91%E4%B8%8A%E7%99%BE%E6%96%B0 %E5%89%B5%E5%9C%98%E9%9A%8A-220100736.html.

20 *See* Tsang, *supra* note 13. On the other hand, according to Jun-Ji Shi, a former Vice Premier, an overbanked environment may be suitable for FinTech startups because they could sell their services or products to incumbent banks that are competing with one another. The situation of overbanking in Taiwan is said to be close to the idea of "monopolistic competition" in which FinTech startups, in a sense, might improve their likelihood of success by cooperating with incumbent banks. Ting-Yu Chang (張庭瑜), *Jin Rong Zheng Bing Li Yu Fin-Tech? Tai Wan Yin Hang Tai Duo Shuo Yin Fa Zheng Fu Dan Wei Bu Tong Tiao* (金融整併利於FinTech？台灣銀行太多說引發政府單位不同調) [*Is the Financial Consolidation Beneficial to FinTech? Government Agencies Have Unaligned Opinions on the Saying that Taiwan's Market is Overbanked*], Shu Wei Shi Dai (數位時代) [Business Next], (Nov. 28, 2017), www.bnext.com.tw/ article/47211/overbanking-fintech-market. In terms of the monopolistic competition, first, sellers could compete with one another by slightly lowering or raising prices based on differentiation of their products; second, buyers might pay the prices including added costs such as those of sales-promotion and of altering products; third, sellers would not win buyers equally in this game, and some of them might earn excessive profits. *Monopoly and Competition*, Encyclopedia Britannica, www.britannica.com/topic/monopoly-economics/Perfect-competition#ref34157 (last visited June 21, 2020).

21 Tsang, *supra* note 13.

22 *See* Purva Khera, Stephanie Ng, Sumiko Ogawa, & Ratna Sahay, *Is Digital Financial Inclusion Unlocking Growth?* 14 (IMF Working Paper, June 2021), https://ssrn.com/abstract=4026364.

23 *See* Cheng-Yun Tsang (臧正運), *Cong Guo Ji Fa Zhan Qu Shi Lun Wo Guo Tui Dong Kai Fang Yin Hang Ying You Zhi Si Kao* (從國際發展趨勢論我國推動開放銀行應有之思考) [*Pondering How to Promote Open Banking in Taiwan from the Perspective of the International Developmental Trend*], 34 Jin Rong Lian He Zheng Xin (金融聯合徵信) [Joint Credit Info. Ctr.] 4, 11–12 (2019). The commentator argued that emphasizing removing only the entry barriers encountered by FinTech startups may not resolve all issues because the market is already overbanked; still, if the products and services provided by banks remain homogeneous, introducing FinTech startups could improve this competitive landscape, ultimately encouraging financial innovation and offering more alternatives to consumers. *Id.* at 11.

24 Navaretti et al., *supra* note 18, at 19.

25 *See* Markos Zachariadis & Pinar Ozcan, *The API Economy and Digital Transformation in Financial Services: The Case of Open Banking* 12 (SWIFT Inst. Working Paper No. 2016–001, June 15, 2017), https://ssrn.com/abstract=2975199

26 *See* Navaretti et al., *supra* note 18, at 19.

27 *See* Tsang, *supra* note 23, at 11.

28 *Ni De Yin Hang Ke Yi Xin Ren Ma? Open Banking Lang Chao Lai Xi Tai Wan Ren Tiao Xuan Yin Hang Zui Zhong Shi San Jian Shi* (你的銀行可以信任嗎? Open Banking浪潮來襲，台灣人挑選銀行最重視三件事) [*Is Your Bank Credible? With Open Banking Coming, What Are Three Things that Taiwanese Care About When Choosing a Bank?*], Ke Ji Bao Ju (科技報橘) [TechOrange], (Apr. 18, 2018), https://buzzorange.com/techorange/2019/04/18/taiwanese-do-not-trust-bank/.

29 *See* Sections 2 and 3.

30 *See* Chapter 3, Section 2.1.1.

31 Tsang, *supra* note 23, at 11–12.

32 *See* Sections 2.1.1, 2.1.5, 2.1.6, and 2.1.7.

33 The term "self-regulatory agency" (the "SRA") is used in studies to refer to the organizations to which the government delegates its law-making powers; hence, they act as the agencies functioning for the principals. Discussions about such delegation would be derived from the relationship between the principal (e.g., the legislature) and the agent (e.g., SRA) theoretically. *See* Ogus, *supra* note 1, at 107; Anthony Ogus, *Self-Regulation*, *in* Encyclopedia of Law & Economics 587, 590–91 (Boudewijn Bouckaert & Gerrit De Geest eds., Edward Elgar Publishing, 1999) (https://doi.org/10.4337/9781782540519.00021). We, however, use a broader term, that is, "SRO," to refer to those self-regulatory bodies.

34 Jing-Yi Li (李靜宜), *Tai Wan Kai Fang Yin Hang Da Jin Zhan! Shou Ban Open API Biao Zhun Chu Lu, 2 Da Zhun Ze 5 Xiang An Kong 13 Jia Yin Hang Xian Zhi Yuan* (臺灣開放銀行大進展！首版Open API標準出爐，2大準則5項安控13家銀行先支援) [*A Huge Improvement in Open Banking in Taiwan! The First Version of Open API Standards Is Released with 2 Main Principles, 5 Safety Controls and 13 Banks' Support.*], iThome, (July 3, 2019), www.ithome.com.tw/news/131648. *See also Zhong Hua Min Guo Yin Hang Gong Hui Hui Yuan Yin Hang Yu Di San Fang Fu Wu Ti Gong Zhe He Zuo Zhi Zi Lü Gui Fan* (中華民國銀行公會會員銀行與第三方服務提供者合作之自律規範) [*The Self-Regulation Governing the Cooperation between Member Banks of the Bankers Association of the Republic of China and Third-Party Services Providers*], art. 1 [hereinafter "OB Self-Regulation"]. The BAROC is assembled mostly by banks, which include 36 commercial banks, 2 industrial banks, 1 export-import bank, and other financial institutions. *History and Functions of the Bankers Association of the Republic of China*, The Bankers Association of the Republic of China, www.ba.org.tw/EnglishVer/Introduction (last visited June 26, 2020).

35 OB Self-Regulation, *supra* note 34, art. 11. In effect, if the self-regulation is backed or approved by a governmental authority, this self-regulation may thus be closer to a form of "co-regulation." Rolf H. Weber, *Sectoral Self-Regulation as Viable Tool*, *in* Law and Economics of Regulation 25, 29–30 (Klaus Mathis & Avishalon Tor eds., 2021) (http://doi.org/10.1007/978-3-030-70530-5_2).

36 *About Us*, The Financial Information Service Co., Ltd., www.fisc.com.tw/EN/ab-history.html (last visited June 26, 2020).

37 Li, *supra* note 34. Since the FISC is delegated by the government to assist in formulating OB rules, it is similar to a quasi-public entity like the OBIE in the UK. Tsang, *supra* note 23, at 12. Arguably, this type of quasi-public entities might be suitable for supporting FinTech-related policies. *See* Yueh-Ping Yang & Chen-Yun Tsang, *RegTech and the New Era of Financial Regulators:*

Envisaging More Public-Private-Partnership Models of Financial Regulators, 21 U. Pa. J. Bus. L. 354, 403 (2018).

38 *Kai Fang API Jia Gou Yu Wei Lai Zhan Wang* (開放API架構與未來展望) [*Open API Framework and Its Prospect*], Cai Jin Gong Si (財金公司) [Fin. Info. Serv. Co., Ltd.], July 7, 2019, at 11, www.ftrc.nccu.edu.tw/wordpresseng/wp-content/uploads/2019/06/2.-%E8%B2%A1%E9%87%91-2019%E9%96%8B%E6%94%BEAPI%E5%89%8D%E7%9E%BB%E6%94%BF%E7%AD%96%E8%88%87%E5%89%B5%E6%96%B0%E6%87%89%E7%94%A8%-E7%A0%94%E8%A8%8E%E6%9C%83.pdf [hereinafter *Open API Framework*, FISC].

See Kai Fang Sheng Tai Xi (開放生態系) [*Open Ecosystem*], FTRC Open Banking, http://openbanking.org.tw/node/60 (last visited Nov. 4, 2019).

39 *Open API Framework*, FISC, *supra* note 38, at 15–16.

40 *See* Li, *supra* note 34.

41 *See* Giuseppe Colangelo & Oscar Borgogno, *Data, Innovation and Transatlantic Competition in Finance: The Case of the Access to Account Rule* 30 (EU L. Working Papers No. 35, 2018), https://www-cdn.law.stanford.edu/wp-content/uploads/2018/09/colangelo_borgogno_eulawpp35.pdf.

42 *Open API Framework*, FISC, *supra* note 38, at 17.

43 *About*, OpenApi Initiative, www.openapis.org/about (last visited Aug. 15, 2019).

44 Xing-Yi Guo (郭幸宜), *Guan Cha: Kai Fang Yin Hang Di Yi Jie Duan 9 Yue Di Shang Xian, 19 Jia Yin Hang Wan Cheng API Yan Zheng* (〈觀察〉開放銀行第一階段9月底上線 19家銀行完成API驗證) [*Observation: Phase 1 of Open Banking Will Be Ready by the End of September, 19 Banks Completed API Authentication*], Ju Heng (鉅亨) [Anue], (Sep. 22, 2019), https://news.cnyes.com/news/id/4385149.

45 *Id.*; Zhong Yang She (中央社), *14 Jin Rong Ji Gou Qiang Kai Fang Yin Hang Tou Xiang Jiao Fei Guan Li Kai Zhi Yi Jian Wan Cheng* (14金融機構搶開放銀行頭香，繳費管理開支一鍵完成) [*14 Financial Institutions Are Competing for Open Banking; Paying and Managing Expenses Can Be Done with One-Click.*], Cai Jing Xin Bao (財經新報) [TechNews], (Aug. 11, 2019), https://finance.technews.tw/2019/08/11/open-banking-api/.

46 Hong-Ren Wang (王宏仁), 【*Kai Fang Yin Hang Te Bie Bao Dao*】 *Cai Jin Kai Fang Api Ping Tai Zhong Yu Shang Lu , 23 Jia Yin Hang Yu 6 Jia Tsp Qiang Xian Bu Ju. Dan Xia Yi Jie Duan Cai Shi Geng Da De Tiao Zhan* (【開放銀行特別報導】財金開放API平臺終於上路，23家銀行與6家TSP搶先布局，但下一階段才是更大的挑戰) [*Special Report on Open Banking: The Open API Platform, Where 23 Banks and 6 TSPs Participate, Is Finally Given, but the Next Phase Is More Challenging.*], iThome, (Oct. 16, 2019), www.ithome.com.tw/news/133650.

47 Guo, *supra* note 44.

48 Jing-Yuan Gao (高敬原), Kai Fang Yin Hang Di Er Jie Duan "Ke Hu Zi Liao Cha Xun," Shen Me Yuan Yin Rang Ge Da Hang Ku Chi Wei Shen Qing? (開放銀行第二階段「客戶資料查詢」，什麼原因讓各大行庫遲未申請？) [*Phase Two of Open Banking – Customers' Account Data: Why Haven't Banks Applied for Joining this Phase?*], Shu Wei Shi Dai (數位時代) [Business Next], (Aug. 5, 2020), www.bnext.com.tw/article/58730/open-banking-second-stage-challenge.

49 Mei-Jun Chen (陳美君), *Kai Fang Yin Hang Mai Bu Jin Ru Di Er Jie Duan* (開放銀行邁步 進入第二階段) [*Open Banking Has Entered Into Its Phase Two.*], Jing Ji Ri Bao (經濟日報) [Economy Daily News], (Nov. 28, 2020), https://money.udn.com/money/story/5613/5049408.

50 Han-Lun Zhu (朱漢崙), *Kai Fang Yin Hang Di Er Jie Duan 10 Jia Can Zhan* (開放銀行第二階段 10家參戰) [*10 Entities Joined the Phase Two of Open Banking.*], Zhong Shi Xin Wen Wang (中時新聞網), (Dec. 1, 2020), www.chinatimes.com/newspapers/20201201000197-260102?chdtv.

51 Zhi-Xuan Chen (陳芝瑄) & Shu-Xian Xia (夏淑賢), *Kai Fang Yin Hang Di Er Jie Duan Fu Wu Shang Xian* (開放銀行第二階段服務上線) [*The Open Banking Services at Phase Two Are Rendered.*], Jing Ji Ri Bao (經濟日報) [Economy Daily News], (Apr. 28, 2021), https://money.udn.com/money/story/5613/5418175.

52 Guo, *supra* note 44.

53 Bi-Fen Chen (陳碧芬), *Kai Fang Yin Hang Di San Jie Duan Jin Du Luo Hou* (開放銀行第三階段 進度落後) [*The Phase Three of Open Banking Is Delayed.*], Gong Shang Shi Bao (工商時報) [Commercial Times], (July 7, 2021), https://readers.ctee.com.tw/cm/20210707/a12aa12/1133722/share; Meng-Lun Wang (王孟倫), *Li Pan Jin Rong Ke Ji Chuang Xin Jin Guan Hui Tui 4 Da Cuo Shi* (力拼金融科技創新 金管會推4大措施) [*Accelerating FinTech Innovation, the FSC Is Implementing 4 Measures.*], Zi You Cai Jing (自由財經) [LTN], (Oct. 4, 2021), https://ec.ltn.com.tw/article/breakingnews/3693042.

54 *See* Chapter 3, Section 2.1.1.

55 Tsang, *supra* note 23, at 10–12.

56 Yu-Yun Huang (黃郁芸), *Jin Guan Hui Jie Lu Kai Fang Yin Hang Jin Zhan, Jiang Ding Api Biao Zhun, Qing Xiang Cai Yong Zi Lü, You Yin Hang Zi Yuan Can Jia* (金管會揭露開放銀行進展, 將定API標準, 傾向採用自律, 由銀行自願參加) [*The FSC Revealed the Progress of OB: API Standards Will be Set, the FSC Inclines to Adopt a Voluntary Approach, and Banks Could Opt In.*], iThome, (Jan. 11, 2019), www.ithome.com.tw/news/128204.

57 *See* Section 1.3.

58 *See* Section 3.

59 *See* Chapter 3, Section 2.1.2.

60 *See Open API Framework*, FISC, *supra* note 38, at 21.

61 *Id.* at 6.

62 Gao, *supra* note 48; Gong Shang Shi Bao (工商時報), *2020 Nian Jin Rong Ke Ji Kai Hua Jie Guo She Lun* (工商社論》2020年金融科技開花結果) [*FinTech Is Flourishing In 2020.*], Zhong Shi Xin Wen Wang (中時新聞網) [China Times], (Jan. 20, 2020), www.chinatimes.com/newspapers/20200120000212-260202?chdtv.

63 *See* Section 1.3; Gao, *supra* note 48.

64 *See* Bi-Fen Chen (陳碧芬), *De Guo Fidor Bank Tai Wan Ke Shi Fa De Kai Fang Yin Hang* (德國Fidor Bank 台灣可師法的開放銀行) [*The German Fidor Bank: A Open Banking Model from Which Taiwan Can Learn Lessons*], Zhong Shi Xin Wen Wang (中時新聞網) [China Times], (Dec. 3, 2018), www.chinatimes.com/newspapers/20181203000217-260202?chdtv. Mobile-only banks are those where banking is able to be done entirely on smartphones and the like. Elizabeth Barry, *Mobile-only banks*, finder (Sep. 27, 2019), www.finder.com.au/mobile-only-banks. They are a type of digital-only banks, which enable users

to access banking services from apps on digital platforms such as smartphones, tablets and the Internet. Infosys, Digital-Only Banking – A Soaring Wave in Consumer Banking 2 (2018), www.infosys.com/industries/financial-services/white-papers/Documents/next-wave-banking.pdf. We use the term "digital-only banks" to refer to a broader meaning.

65 "BaaP" indicates that banks would turn to the adoption of a platform business model. *See* Zachariadis & Ozcan, *supra* note 25, at 4, 11. Therefore, banking services could be delivered through platforms; consequently, more alternatives to access to banking services are provided. Vinod Sharma, *Fintech: The BaaP and BaaS Boomer*, Finextra (Mar. 30, 2016), www.finextra.com/blogposting/12414/fintech-the-baap-and-baas-boomer. *See also* Patricia Hines, Celent, APIs in Banking: Unlocking Business Value with Banking as a Platform (BaaP) 6 (Mar. 21, 2018), www.fidor.com/documents/analyst-reports/celent-apis-in-banking-unlocking-business-value-with-baap.PDF (noting that BaaP "occurs when a bank acts as an infrastructure provider to external third parties.").

66 *See id.* at 6, 11–19.

67 As for whether the regulatory policies are capable of doing so in the context of OB in Taiwan, *see* Section 3.

68 In 2021 in which the ESVC Act (as further introduced in *infra* note 69 and accompanying text) was merged into the Act Governing Electronic Payment Institutions (hereinafter the "EPI Act"), according to the current EPI Act, "electronic payment institutions" are the approved companies operating businesses such as (1) acting as an agent collecting and making payments for real transactions, (2) receiving stored funds, (3) domestic and foreign small amount remittance business, (4) the business related to the above three businesses and involving buying or selling currencies issued by Mainland China, Hong Kong, or Macao, or (4) other related businesses. *Dian Zi Zhi Fu Ji Gou Guan Li Tiao Li* (電子支付機構管理條例) [*Act Governing Electronic Payment Institutions*], art. 3, para. 1, subpara. 1; art. 4, para. 1 and para. 2. In addition, an electronic payment institution shall have a minimum pain-in capital of NTD 500 million. Nevertheless, the institutions that engage in neither receiving stored funds nor domestic and foreign small amount remittances business can have a lower minimum pain-in capital of NTD 100 million. *Id.*, art. 9, para. 1, subpara. 1. The institutions that do not engage in foreign small amount remittances business can have a lower minimum pain-in capital of NTD 300 million. *Id.*, art. 9, para. 1, subpara. 2. Further, a similar type of institutions is companies engaging in third-party payment, but they are excluded from the definition of electronic payment institution under Art. 5, Para. 1, Subpapa. 2 of the EPI Act. They act only as an agent in collecting and making payments for real transactions, and the total amount of funds shall be less than NTD 2 billion. *Dian Zi Zhi Fu Ji Gou Guan Li Tiao Li Di Wu Tiao Di Er Xiang Shou Quan Gui Ding Shi Xiang Ban Fa* (電子支付機構管理條例第五條第二項授權規定事項辦法) [*Regulations Regarding Paragraph 2, Article 5 of the Act Governing Electronic Payment Institutions*], art. 3.

69 Before the merger into the EPI Act in 2021, according to the then Act Governing Issuance of Electronic Stored Value Cards (hereinafter the "ESVC Act"), "electronic stored value card issuers" are the approved companies issuing the instruments such as IC chips, cards, certificates applying electronic, magnetic or optical means to store monetary value for payment purposes. *Dian Zi Piao Zheng Fa Xing Guan Li Tiao Li* (電子票證發行管理條例) [*Act Governing*

Issuance of Electronic Stored Value Cards], art. 3, para. 1, subpara. 1 & subpara. 2. The minimum paid-in capital is NTD 300 million. *Id.*, art. 6, para. 1. The competent authority for electronic stored value card issuers is the FSC. *Id.*, art. 2. The aforementioned two statutes, that is, the EPI Act and ESVC Act, had been scheduled in 2019 to be merged together, with the former remaining as the governing law. Zhen-Ling Peng (彭禎伶) & Qiao-Yi Wei (魏喬怡), *Dian Zhi Dian Piao Er He Yi, Jin Guan Hui: Xin Zeng Si Da Xiao Yi* (電支電票二合一 金管會：新增四大效益) [*The Act Governing Electronic Payment Institutions and the Act Governing Issuance of Electronic Stored Value Cards Will Be Merged; the FSC: Four Benefits Are About to Be Reaped*], Zhong Shi Xin Wen Wang (中時新聞網) [China Times], (July 31, 2019), www.chinatimes.com/ newspapers/20190731000269-260205?chdtv. On December 25, 2020, it was announced that the ESVC Act has been merged into the EPI Act. Jin Guan Hui (金管會) [FSC], *Li Fa Yuan San Du Tong Guo "Dian Zi Zhi Fu Ji Gou Guan Li Tiao Li" Xiu Zheng An* (立法院三讀通過「電子支付機構管理條例」修正 案) [*The Amendment to the Act Governing Electronic Payment Institutions Was Approved by the Legislative Yuan*], (Dec. 25, 2020), www.fsc.gov.tw/ch/home. jsp?id=96&parentpath=0,2&mcustomize=news_view.jsp&dataserno=202012 250002&dtable=News. The merger between the EPI Act and ESVC Act was officially promulgated and the amendment to the EPI Act took effect in 2021; as for detailed comments on the newly-amended EPI Act, *see generally* Yu-Ting Lin (林育廷), *Cong Xia Pi Shi Jian Chu Ping 2021 Dian Zi Zhi Fu Ji Gou Guan Li Tiao Li Zhi Xiu Zheng* (從蝦皮事件初評2021電子支付機構管理條例之修 正) [*Preliminary Commentary on the 2021 Amendment to the Act Governing Electronic Payment Institutions: A Perspective from the Shoppee Saga*], 321 Yue Dan Fa Xue Za Zhi (月旦法學雜誌) [Taiwan Law Review] 183, 183–202 (2022). After the merger between the EPI Act and the ESVC Act, under the new EPI Act, the electronic payment institutions could be electronic stored value card issuers under the old ESVC Act, that is, the entities accepting deposited funds in advance and engaging in using an electronic payment account or a stored value card for payments. *Act Governing Electronic Payment Institutions*, *supra* note 68, art. 3, para. 1, subpara. 7. The minimum required capital for this type of electronic payment institutions remains NTD 300 million. *Id.*, art. 9, para. 1, subpara. 2.

70 *Zhong Hua Min Guo Yin Hang Gong Hui Hui Yuan Yin Hang Yu Di San Fang Fu Wu Ti Gong Zhe He Zuo Zhi Zi Lü Gui Fan Cao An Ji Shuo Ming* (中華民 國銀行公會會員銀行與第三方服務提供者合作之自律規範」草案及說明) [*Explanation for and the Draft of the Self-Regulation Governing the Cooperation between Member Banks of the Bankers Association of the Republic of China and Third-Party Services Providers*], art. 3 [hereinafter Draft of the Self-Regulation Governing OB in Taiwan] (noting that the official comment of this article gives these four examples of TSPs).

71 *See* Section 2.1.7.

72 *See* Section 3.1.

73 *See* Section 1.3.

74 Jing-Yuan Gao (高敬原), *Kai Fang Yin Hang Di Yi Jie Duan Yue Di Shang Xian, Yin Hang Ye Tan Yan: Chu Qi Xiao Fei Zhe Gan Shou Bu Da* (開放銀 行第一階段月底上線，銀行業坦言：初期消費者感受不大) [*Phase One of Open Banking Will Get Started at the End of this Month; the Banking Industry Frankly Expresses that Consumers May Not Enjoy Great Benefits in the Very*

Beginning], Shu Wei Shi Dai (數位時代) [Business Next], (Sep. 23, 2019), www.bnext.com.tw/article/54847/taiwan-open-banking-step-one

75 Tsang, *supra* note 23, at 11.

76 *See* Editorial Team, *Kai Fang Yin Hang Yu Xiao Fei Zhe Fu Quan De Xiang Xiang Ji Tiao Zhan* (開放銀行與消費者賦權的想像及挑戰) [*Imagination and Challenges of Open Banking and Consumer Empowerment*], Tai Wan Ren Gong Zhi Hui Xing Dong Wang (臺灣人工智慧行動網) [Taiwan Artificial Intelligence Wise Agent Network], (Oct. 23, 2020), https://ai.iias.sinica.edu.tw/open-bank-business/.

77 *See* Tsang, *supra* note 23, at 11.

78 *See* Chapter 3, Section 2.1.4.

79 Gao, *supra* note 48.

80 Hong-Da Chen (陳鴻達), *Kai Fang Yin Hang Yao "Shu Tong Wen, Che Tong Gui" Ma? Shen Me Shi Tai Wan Zui Shi He De Mo Shi* (開放銀行要「書同文、車同軌」嗎？什麼是台灣最適合的模式) [*Is It Necessary to "Standardize Languages and Machines" When Open Banking? What Is the Most Suitable Approach for Taiwan?*], Shu Wei Shi Dai (數位時代) [Business Next], (Dec. 30, 2019), www.bnext.com.tw/article/56103/open-banking-mode-taiwan.

81 *Open API Framework*, FISC, *supra* note 38, at 10–11.

82 *Id.*

83 *Kai Fang API Ye Wu Fen Xiang* (「開放API」業務分享) [*Sharing of "Open API" Business*], Cai Jin Gong Si (財金公司) [Fin. Info. Serv. Co., Ltd.], (Sep. 18, 2019), www.ftrc.nccu.edu.tw/wordpresseng/wp-content/uploads/2019/09/20190918-%E8%B2%A1%E9%87%91%E5%85%AC%E5%8F%B8-%E6%A5%AD%E5%8B%99%E5%88%86%E4%BA%AB%E7%9A%A1%E5%A0%B1-V.6F.pdf [hereinafter *Open API Business Sharing*].

84 Editorial Team, *supra* note 76.

85 *See* Cheng-Yun Tsang (臧正運), *Kai Fang Yin Hang De Guan Jian Tiao Zhan Di San Fang Fu Wu Ti Gong Zhe Zhi Zhi Li Mo Shi Xuan Ze* (開放銀行的關鍵挑戰 第三方服務提供者之治理模式選擇) [*The Critical Challenge of Open Banking: How to Choose Among the Governance Modes of Third-Party Service Providers.*], 97 Cai Jin Zi Xun Ji Kan (財金資訊季刊) [Journal of Financial Information Quarterly] 8, 14 (2020).

86 *See* Nai-Ren Yang (楊酒仁), *Kai Fang Yin Hang Mai Xiang Di Er Jie Duan-Open Api Ji Shu Ge Gui Yu Ce Shi Shuo Ming Hui* (開放銀行邁向第二階段－－OPEN API技術合規與測試說明會) [*Open Banking Is Proceeding to Phase Two – Seminar on Open API Technical Compliance and Trial Explanations.*], CIO Taiwan, (July 1, 2020), www.cio.com.tw/open-bank-towards-phase-2-open-api-technical-compliance-and-test-description/.

87 *See Open API Framework*, FISC, *supra* note 38, at 11, 13. The external consultants including scholars and outside experts are invited to participate in the process of determining open API standards, by assisting in checking the suitability, readability, and accuracy of such standards. *Id.* at 10.

88 Ruo-Pu Wang (王若樸), *Jin Guan Hui: Kai Fang Yin Hang Zheng Ce Jiang Cai Zi Yuan Zi Lu Zhi* (金管會：開放銀行政策將採自願自律制) [*A Voluntary Self-Regulatory Policy Will Be Adopted to Promote Open Banking*], iThome, (Jan. 19, 2019), www.ithome.com.tw/news/128317 (highlighting that in a public hearing of the Legislature, this commentator together with others used to argue that before implementing OB policies, not only banks but also FinTech firms, users, and scholars should be invited to participate in the process of setting common API standards).

89 OB Self-Regulation, *supra* note 34, art. 4, para. 1, sub-paras. 2 & 3.
90 *See* Peng, *supra* note 5; OB Self-Regulation, *supra* note 34, art. 10, para. 2.
91 *See* Section 2.1.3.
92 OB Self-Regulation, *supra* note 34, art. 4, para. 1, sub-paras. 2 & 3.
93 *Id.* art. 5, para. 1, sub-para. 5.
94 Ding-Min Lin (林鼎閔), *Tai Wan Open Banking Jin Kuang Fa Zhan* (臺灣 Open Banking近況發展) [*Recent Development and Progress of the Open Banking in Taiwan.*], Money, (Mar. 3, 2020), www.moneynet.com.tw/article /10295/%E8%87%BA%E7%81%A3OpenBanking%E8%BF%91%E6%B3% 81%E7%99%BC%E5%B1%95.
95 *See* Chapter 3, Sections 2.1.3, and 2.1.7.
96 *See* Chapter 3, Section 2.1.7.
97 *See* Peggy Valcke, Niels Vandezande, & Nathan Van de Velde, *The Evolution of Third Party Payment Providers and Cryptocurrencies under the EU's Upcoming PSD2 and AMLD4* 17–18 (SWIFT Inst. Working Paper No. 2015–001, 2015), http://ssrn.com/abstract=2665973; EBA, *Final Report on the EBA Guidelines under Directive (EU) 2015/2366 (PSD2) on the Information to Be Provided for the Authorisation of Payment Institutions and E-money Institutions and for the Registration of Account Information Service Providers* 9 (2017), https://eba.europa.eu/sites/default/documents/files/documents/10180/1904583/f0e94433-f59b-4c24-9cec-2d6a2277b62c/Final%20 Guidelines%20on%20Authorisations%20of%20Payment%20Institutions%20 (EBA-GL-2017-09).pdf.
98 The account information in the UK and EU seems to be similar to the information opened up in phases two and three in Taiwan. *See* Chapter 3, Section 2.1.4.
99 *See* Section 2.1.6.
100 *See* Chapter 2, Sections 1 and 2.1.
101 *See* EBA Open Banking Working Group, *Open Banking: Advancing Customer-centricity – Analysis and Overview* 19–20 (Mar. 2017).
102 In modern finance where sharing of information or data is crucial for enhancing market efficiency, payment services regulation, such as OB regulations, concerning the sharing of information or data should be considered when improving the consumer credit reporting system, which is also based on information or data sharing. *See* Nikita Aggarwal, *Big Data and the Obsolescence of Consumer Credit Reports*, Oxford Bus. L. Blog (July 15, 2019), www.law.ox.ac.uk/business-law-blog/blog/2019/07/ big-data-and-obsolescence-consumer-credit-reports.
103 *See* Section 2.1.
104 Chang-Hsien Tsai, Ching-Fu Lin, & Han-Wei Liu, *The Diffusion of the Sandbox Approach to Disruptive Innovation and Its Limitations*, 53 Cornell Int'l L. J. 261, 284; Chang-Hsien Tsai, *To Regulate or Not to Regulate? A Comparison of Government Responses to Peer-to-Peer Lending among the United States, China, and Taiwan*, 87 U. Cin. L. Rev. 1077, 1118–19 (2019).
105 Tsai et al., *supra* note 104, at 291–92.
106 *Jin Rong Ke Ji Fa Zhan Yu Chuang Xin Shi Yan Tiao Li* (金融科技發展與 創新實驗條例) [*Financial Technology Development and Innovative Experimentation Act*] (hereinafter the "FinTech Sandbox Act"), art. 1. The FinTech Sandbox Act became effective on January 31, 2018.
107 Tsai et al., *supra* note 104, at 293–95. Therefore, even if the FinTech Sandbox Act was enacted as a potential regulatory-design solution to achieving public interest goals (i.e., promoting financial competition, innovation, and inclusion),

the FSC's overly conservative implementation might render this solution ineffective. *See* Ogus, *supra* note 1, at 71 (explaining that "an appropriate regulatory design may have been rendered ineffectual by inadequate enforcement, whether that resulted from the relevant agency lacking insufficient resources or adopting a passive, compromising approach to contraventions.").

108 *Id.* at 25–26. To examine three American banks used as examples of bank-FinTech partnership under the current regulatory system in the United States that demonstrate the potential to expand financial inclusion, *see* Joseph Caputo & Lee Reiners, *The Rise of Rent-A-Charter: Examining New Risks Behind Bank-FinTech Partnerships*, The FinReg Blog (Jan. 23, 2020), https://sites.law.duke. edu/thefinregblog/2020/01/23/the-rise-of-rent-a-charter-examining-new-risks-behind-bank-fintech-partnerships/. Commentators used to argue that chances that FinTech startups could test their innovations might be relatively limited in regulatory sandboxes; however, within an "innovation hub's" regulatory regime—where FinTech firms could easily access regulators—testing innovation would be easier. *See* Ross P. Buckley, Douglas Arner, Robin Veidt & Dirk Zetzsche, *Building FinTech Ecosystems: Regulatory Sandboxes, Innovation Hubs and Beyond* 5, 26–27 (UNSW Research Paper No. 19–72, 2019), https:// ssrn.com/abstract=3455872 (highlighting that "[a] sandbox and/or an innovation hub are designed to promote innovation and competition.").

109 Jing-Yi Li (李靜宜), *Jin Guan Hui Jiang Kai Fang Chun Wang Bao Xu You Jin Rong Ji Gou Yu FinTech Gong Si Gong Tong Fa Qi. Zui Kua 2023 Nian Gong Bu She Li Xu Ke Ming Dan* (金管會將開放純網保！需由金融機構與Fintech公司共同發起，最快2023年公布設立許可名單) [*The FSC Will Allow Online Insurance! Such an Insurance Entity Needs to Be Established by Both a Financial Institution and a FinTech Company. The Allowing List Will be Announced in 2023 as the Soonest.*], iThome, (Dec. 21, 2021), www. ithome.com.tw/news/148491.

110 For instance, both the equity crowdfunding ("ECF") regulations governing the public and private platforms in Taiwan were formed in 2014 and 2015, respectively, after the US Title III of the JOBS Act in 2012 (i.e., the so-called "CROWDFUND Act") and adapted to local conditions. The aforementioned ECF regulatory trajectory may illustrate a conservative regulatory approach to emerging FinTech during the early stage of the market's development in Taiwan. *See generally* Chang-Hsien Tsai, *Is a Bird in the Hand Worth Two in the Bush? Reflections on Equity Crowdfunding Regulation in Taiwan, in* Research Handbook on Asian Financial Law 525 (Douglas W. Arner et al. eds., Edward Elgar Publishing, 2020) (http://doi.org/10.4337/9781788972208.00037).

111 Tsai, *supra* note 104, at 1082, 1118.

112 *Id.* at 1081–82; Tsai et al., *supra* note 104, at 284–85.

113 Tsai, *supra* note 104, at 1118. In addition to their risk-averse tendency, which limits the effectiveness of regulations, regulators' avoidance behavior may result in poor policy analysis. Ogus, *supra* note 1, at 56. However, in the context of OB policies in Taiwan, this book highlights the regulators' conservativeness in a broader sense, including their risk-averse tendencies and avoidance behaviors.

114 As of April 2020, it was reported that only seven experiments—in which the testing firms are still traditional financial institutions, rather than FinTech firms initially envisioned—have been approved and conducted. Guo-Rui Chen (陳國瑞), *"Jin Rong Jian Li Sha He" Shang Lu Liang Nian Zhi He Zhun Qi*

An, Wen Ti Chu Zai Na Li? (「金融監理沙盒」上路兩年只核准七案，問題出在哪裡？) [*Only 7 Experiments Have Been Approved Since the FinTech Sandbox Kicked off for 2 Years; what Are the Problems?*], Guan Jian Ping Lun (關鍵評論) [The News Lens], (Apr. 24, 2020), www.thenewslens.com/article/134230.

115 Regarding how the FSC's implementation of the FinTech Sandbox Act exemplifies the potential regulatory pitfalls, *see* Section 3.1.

116 *See* Hakan Eroglu, *The Asia-Pacific Way of Open Banking Regulation*, Finextra (June 20, 2019), www.finextra.com/blogposting/17396/the-asia-pacific-way-of-open-banking-regulation.

117 BNP Paribas, *World Payments Report 2018*, at 38–39 (2018), https://worldpaymentsreport.com/wp-content/uploads/sites/5/2018/10/World-Payments-Report-2018.pdf.

118 *Id.* at 38; Eroglu, *supra* note 116; Graham Rothwell, *The Brave New World of Open Banking in APAC: Singapore*, Accenture (Sep. 27, 2018), https://bankingblog.accenture.com/brave-new-world-open-banking-apac-singapore?lang=en_US; ABS-MAS, Finance-as-a-Service: API Playbook 9 (2016), https://abs.org.sg/docs/library/abs-api-playbook.pdf.

119 Emma Leong, *Open Banking: The Changing Nature of Regulating Data – A Case Study of Australia and Singapore*, 35 Bank. & Fin. L. Rev. 443, 447 (2020).

120 *Open Application Programming Interface (API) for the Banking Sector*, Hong Kong Monetary Authority, www.hkma.gov.hk/eng/key-functions/international-financial-centre/open-api-for-banking-sector.shtml (last visited Sep. 7, 2019).

121 Jing-Yuan Gao (高敬原), *Zeng Bei Pi Zha Pian Ji Tuan, Zao Yin Hang Jie Feng Sha, Ma Bu Ji Zhang App Ru He Da Shang Kai Fang Yin Hang Feng Chao Chong Sheng?* (曾被批詐騙集團、遭銀行界封殺，麻布記帳App如何搭上開放銀行風潮重生?) [*Once Criticized as Fraudulent and Blocked by the Banking Industry, How Was Moneybook App Reborn during the Trend of Open Banking?*], Shu Wei Shi Dai (數位時代) [Business Next], (July 25, 2019), www.bnext.com.tw/article/54107/moneybook.

122 *See* Tsang, *supra* note 23, at 6–7, 9–12; Wang, *supra* note 88 (reporting that in the public hearing of the Legislature before the determination of OB policies, the FSC sided with banks to expressly support the voluntary approach to Open API adopted in Singapore and Hong Kong whereas FinTech firms argued for the UK's compulsory approach to OB).

123 According to a former Taiwanese legislator specializing in FinTech issues, the FSC was "finally catching up on the global trend and [started] envisaging the development of 'open banking' in Taiwan" after it had fallen behind this trend. *See* Karen Yu, *4 Reasons Why Taiwan Should Pursue Compulsory "Open Banking,"* Medium (Jan. 18, 2019), https://medium.com/datadriveninvestor/4-reasons-why-taiwan-should-pursue-compulsory-open-banking-b9528ae-9cf0a. More importantly, she agrees with this book's contention that promoting OB in a compulsory fashion would benefit FinTech innovation and competition, ultimately benefiting financial inclusion, stating that "pursuing compulsory open banking bodes well to the long-term development of Taiwan's Fintech industry" and "[m]ore resources would be devoted to Fintech start-ups, which can offer better and cheaper financial services to the public, making financial services more inclusive." *Id.*

124 BNP Paribas, *supra* note 117, at 23.

125 Factors determining payment system evolution embrace supply-side push and demand-side pull; when the regulatory supply-side push is "reactive and patchy" and the demand-side pull requests E-payments products, this would contribute to a scenario where the demand-side pull leads the evolution of the market because customers enthusiastically desire to use FinTech-based payment methods while the regulator is more reactive. *See* BNP Paribas, *supra* note 117, at 14. *See also id.*, at 23–24 (highlighting that "[p]roactive countries such as Singapore, Australia, the UK and Sweden have proactive regulators and enthusiastic demand-side institutions that are ready to embrace regulatory initiatives.").

126 *See, for example*, Pei-Hua Lu (盧沛樺), *Xu Ni Huo Bi Yu Lai Yu Nan Wan? Wei Lai Fan Xi Qian Xin Gui Shang Lu, Xian Guo Jin Guan Hui Zhe Guan!* (虛擬貨幣愈來愈難玩？未來反洗錢新規上路，先過金管會這關！) [*Harder to Carry on the Virtual Currency Transactions? With New Anti-Money Laundering Regulation Taking Effect in the Future, Dealers Need Tackle the Task First Set by the FSC!*], Tian Xia Za Zhi (天下雜誌) [CommonWealth Magazine], (July 4, 2019), www.cw.com.tw/article/5095892?template=transformers; Qiao-Yi Wei (魏喬怡) & Zhen-Ling Peng (彭禎伶), *Jin Rong Ke Ji Ye Zhe Qiu Zhe Liang Yang Xue Zhe Xia Dao* (金融科技業者求這兩樣 學者嚇到) [*Scholars Were Surprised that FinTech Firms Made these Two Requests.*], Gong Shang Shi Bao (工商時報) [Commercial Times], (June 17, 2020), https://m.ctee.com.tw/livenews/aj/a95645002020061719573007?area=.

127 *See* P. N. Grabosky, *Regulation by Reward: On the Use of Incentives as Regulatory Instruments*, 17 Law & Pol'y 257, 261 (1995).

128 The unwillingness of opening data pools may mirror this notion. *See* Section 1.3.

129 Marver H. Bernstein, *Regulating Business by Independent Commission* 251 (1955) (http://doi.org/10.1515/9781400878789).

130 *See* BNP Paribas, *supra* note 117, at 23–24.

131 *See* Tsai, *supra* note 104, at 1082, 1118–19. Regulatory inertia refers to a regulator's tendency to follow extant rules rather than to make changes to the rules in order to achieve a more desirable outcome. *See* Asaf Eckstein, *Regulatory Inertia and Interest Groups: How the Structure of the Rulemaking Process Affects the Substance of Regulations* 3 (2015), https://ssrn.com/abstract=2285593.

132 It is the same case with peer-to-peer lending ("P2P lending") in Taiwan, since the FSC also required the BAROC to draft self-regulatory rules to encourage collaboration between banks and P2P lending platforms. Tsai, *supra* note 104, at 1103. In general, regulations for P2P lending platforms are worth examining as the rise of these platforms are regarded as one of the transformations stemming from FinTech. Moran Ofir & Ido Sadeh, *The Rise of FinTech: Promises, Perils and Challenges* 11–12 (2021), https://ssrn.com/abstract=3788168.

133 *See* Section 2.1.5.

134 *See* Section 2.1.6.

135 *See* Section 2.1.7.

136 *See* Rory Van Loo, *Making Innovation More Competitive: The Case of FinTech*, 65 UCLA L. Rev. 232, 259 (2018) (arguing that due to mission conflict and avoiding threats to banks' profitability and or safety and soundness, the U.S. OCC encouraged "bank-fintech partnerships" because "it lacks the institutional incentive to divert its resources away from safety and soundness

monitoring to developing fintech licenses."). This "mission conflict" explanation might apply to the FSC's promotion of bank-TSP partnerships as the voluntary approach to OB in Taiwan as well. *See* Section 3.4. In contrast of this book's darker view on bank-FinTech partnerships due to regulatory capture and inertia, on advocating for a brighter side of Bank-FinTech partnerships, *see generally* Luca Enriques & Wolf-Georg Ringe, *Bank-Fintech Partnerships, Outsourcing Arrangements and the Case for a Mentorship Regime* (European Corporate Governance Institute (ECGI)—Law Working Paper No. 527/2020, 2020), https://ssrn.com/abstract=3625578.

137 *See* Peng, *supra* note 5; Yi-Shan Chen (陳一姍), *Cong Bei Ji Cun Zheng Xin Han Dao Qiang Zhe He Zuo Ma Bu Ji Zhang Ru He Bian Cheng 25 Jia Yin Hang De Zui Ai?* (從被寄存證信函到搶著合作，麻布記帳如何變成25家銀行的最愛？) [*From Being Warned by Banks via Lawyer's Letters to Being Competed among Banks for Cooperation: How Would Moneybook Turn Darling Partners of 25 Banks?*], Tian Xia Za Zhi (天下雜誌) [CommonWealth Magazine], (Oct. 28, 2019), www.cw.com.tw/article/5097409?template=trans formers&utm_campaign=Daily&utm_medium=referral&utm_source=rss_htc (illustrating the FSC's implicit requirement for cooperation and collaboration between banks and Fintech firms as a precondition for the latter to enter the financial market).

138 *See* Section 2.1.7 and Chapter 3, Section 2.1.3.

139 *See* Chapter 3, Section 2.1.7.

140 *See* Section 2.1.3.

141 *See* Section 2.1.7.

142 The competent authority for electronic payment institutions and for electronic stored value card issuers is the FSC, whereas that for the companies engaging in third-party payments is the ministry of economic affairs. *See supra* notes 68, 69, and accompanying text.

143 *See* Kun-Zheng Lin (林坤正), *Lin Kun Zheng: Tai Wan Li Kai Fang Yin Hang Hai Hen Yuan* (林坤正：台灣離開放銀行還很遠!) [*Kun-Zheng Lin: It's Still a Long Way for Taiwan to Attain the Aim of Open Banking!*], Cai Xun (財訊) [Wealth Magazine], (Mar. 21, 2019), www.wealth.com.tw/ home/articles/20149. *See also* Nissim Cohen & Hadar Yoana Jabotinsky, *Nudge Regulation and Innovation Policy* 9 (Jan. 22, 2020), https://ssrn.com/ abstract=3523910 (noting that "old solutions and incremental changes are not necessarily the best strategy in policy design.").

144 *See* Eroglu, *supra* note 116.

145 *Id.* Even in Singapore, a pioneer of promoting OB in FinTech development, we can observe a similar stubborn dependence in the case of competition for digital banking license. *See* Yoolim Lee & Chanyaporn Chanjaroen, *Singapore Fintech Startup Abandons Plans Competing for Digital Banking License*, Bloomberg (Nov. 5, 2019), www.bloomberg.com/news/ articles/2019-11-05/rebranded-instarem-abandons-singapore-digital-banking-race (last visited Nov. 15, 2019).

146 Yao-Lian Cao (蔡曜蓮) & Wei-Xuan Huang (黃煒軒), *Jin Rong Ke Ji Yao Kua Bu Zou, Jin Guan Hui Bu Ying Guo Du Pian Xin Yin Hang Ye* (金融科技要跨步走 金管會不應過度偏心銀行業) [*Financial Technology Could Develop Further Only When the FSC Would Avoid Acting in Favor of the Banking Industry Unduly.*], Jin Zhou Kan (今周刊) [Business Today], (Mar. 29, 2019), www.businesstoday.com.tw/article/category/80392/post/201903290004/%

E9%87%91%E8%9E%8D%E7%A7%91%E6%8A%80%E8%A6%81%
E8%B7%A8%E6%AD%A5%E8%B5%B0%20%E9%87%91%E7%AE%
A1%E6%9C%83%E4%B8%8D%E6%87%89%E9%81%8E%E5%BA%A
6%E5%81%8F%E5%BF%83%E9%8A%80%E8%A1%8C%E6%A5%AD.
See also Tsai et al., *supra* note 104, at 285–87.

147 Peculiarly, public interest goals underlying this regulation could not be achieved because regulatory agencies are subverted, influenced, and even bribed. Thus, the interests of those who are supposed to be subject to the regulation are protected. Ogus, *supra* note 1, at 57.

148 *See* Tsai, *supra* note 104, at 1121; Chang-Hsien Tsai, *Choosing Among Authorities for Consumer Financial Protection in Taiwan*, in The Political Economy of Financial Regulation 219, 241–44 (Emilios Avgouleas & David C. Donald eds., Cambridge University Press, 2019) (http://doi.org/10.1017/9781108612821.009). Asking a prudential regulator, whose focus is stability, to simultaneously handle FinTech development and promotion of innovation and competition may result in mission conflicts. *See* Van Loo, *supra* note 136, at 259, 273–75.

149 Rachel E. Barkow, *Insulating Agencies: Avoiding Capture Through Institutional Design*, 89 Tex. L. Rev. 15, 50 (2010).

150 *See* Sections 3.1 and 3.2.

151 *See*, for example, Samuel Weinstein, *Blockchain Neutrality*, Ga. L. Rev. (forthcoming, 2020) (manuscript at 6–8), https://ssrn.com/abstract=3540537 (highlighting that even if being statutorily mandated to promote competition, in coping with blockchain-related competition, sector regulators such as "the SEC and CFTC strongly favor consumer safety and systemic risk prevention over competition concerns," that "their focus to date has been on fraud prevention and classification and registration of financial products and entities," and that "the agencies should be thinking systematically about how to encourage block-based competition . . . [because a] narrow focus on fraud and registration requirements misses the forest for the trees."). In addition, a commentator argued that blockchain technology transactions could be regulated by defining asset classes in private laws. Heather Hughes, *The Complex Implications of FinTech for Financial Inclusion*, 84 L. & Contemp. Probl. 113, 124 (2021). Overall, looking into the nature of FinTech and understanding its complexity are pivotal when dealing with the risks it produces while trying to achieve financial inclusion. *See id.* at 122–23, 126.

152 *See* Barkow, *supra* note 149, at 50; Samuel N. Weinstein, *Financial Regulation in the (Receding) Shadow of Antitrust*, 91 Temp. L. Rev. 447, 452 (2019) (noting that "[c]apture of sector regulators also is a concern and may reduce incentives for agencies to undertake actions against the best interests of bigger firms in regulated markets, including promoting competition from new entrants or smaller players," and, thus, that "competition in financial markets may suffer as antitrust is displaced by regulations enforced by agencies poorly suited to the task of preserving and promoting competitive markets.").

153 *See* Tsai et al., *supra* note 104, at 284–86; Tsai, *supra* note 104, at 1082.

154 When it comes to how a captured regulator is faced with new technologies like FinTech, since the legacy industry has more information than the regulator, "the regulators have almost no choice but to consult with the industry and rely heavily on its explanations. Thus, the regulators tend to frequently adopt regulatory solutions suggested by the industry itself without questioning

them further." Cohen & Jabotinsky, *supra* note 143, at 17 (footnote omitted). *See also* Peng, *supra* note 5 (describing how the FSC directed BAROC to research whether Taiwan should adopt the UK's mandatory approach to OB or the voluntary one adopted in Singapore or Hong Kong, and that the FSC in 2019 indicated its preference for adopting the voluntary self-regulatory model to avoid banks' backlash against OB promotion).

155 Wan-Ru Yu (余宛如), *Ban Le 15 Chang Jin Rong Ke Ji Zuo Tan Hui, Tai Wan FinTech Jiu Neng Qi Fei?* (辦了15場金融科技座談會，台灣FinTech就能起 飛?) [*Can 15 FinTech Conferences Help the FinTech in Taiwan Soar?*], Tu Na Shang Ye Ping Lun (吐納商業評論) [Tuna Business Review], (Sep. 14, 2016), https://tuna.press/?p=4039.

156 Jie-Yu Li (黎婕妤), *Gu Li Xiong Wa Jie "Cai Jin Bang," Jin Guan Hui Guan Yuan Tui Xiu Jin Ren Gong Gu Dai Biao* (顧立雄瓦解「財金幫」金管會官 員退休禁任公股代表) [*Li-Xiong Gu Disrupted the "Finance Group": Officials Retiring from the FSC Are Not Allowed to Serve as Government's Representatives of State-Owned Enterprises*], Jin Zhou Kan (今周刊) [Business Today], (May 23, 2018), www.businesstoday.com.tw/article/category/80392/ post/201805230034/%E9%A1%A7%E7%AB%8B%E9%9B%84%E7%93% A6%E8%A7%A3%E3%80%8C%E8%B2%A1%E9%87%91%E5%B9%A B%E3%80%8D%20%E9%87%91%E7%AE%A1%E6%9C%83%E5%AE%- 98%E5%93%A1%E9%80%80%E4%BC%91%E7%A6%81%E4%BB%BB %E5%85%AC%E8%82%A1%E4%BB%A3%E8%A1%A8. Theoretical support confirms that interest groups' employing governmental officials is one way in which private interests influence political decisions including the formation of regulation. Ogus, *supra* note 1, at 70.

157 The drafting process of the PSD2 and the EBA's draft RTS is informative in illustrating why it would be preferable to adopt a compulsory approach to OB for "the competent financial regulators to ensure that the Fintech companies whose activities are covered by the PSD2 are not blocked or obstructed in the provision of their services." Simonetta Vezzoso, *Fintech, Access to Data, and the Role of Competition Policy, in* Competition and Innovation 30, 37 (V. Bagnoli ed., 2018) (https://dx.doi.org/10.2139/ssrn.3106594). Specifically, to illustrate how "the devil likes to dwell in complex technical details" to prevent banks' undue influence in the flow of data to FinTech firms,

[d]uring the drafting of the Directive, Fintech companies put forth the argument that, under the PDS2, direct access to customer account data, as alternative to the dedicated interface provided by the *banks*, would have been essential to prevent strategic obstacles to the data flow. A key concern was that the banks' control over the (proprietary) dedicated interfaces would have given them ample scope for ring-fencing the customer's account data . . .. In the EBA's draft RTS published at the beginning of 2017, the access to the customer's account data via the "normal" customer facing interfaces (i.e., via the online *banking* portal), albeit "adapted," was supplemented by the alternative option of the provision of a dedicated interface. In this way, the information would have been transferred to the Fintech company not directly but via the *bank*'s dedicated interface. This raised concerns, also among national competition authorities, that *banks* could exploit the new leeway by hampering the flow of information toward Fintech companies, undermining consumer trust and interest in these new services.

Id. at 35–36 (emphasis added) (footnote omitted).

158 *See* Ogus, *supra* note 1, at 155 (highlighting that "the imposition of more stringent standards on 'newer' firms may create barriers to entry and thus protect 'older' firms from competition").

159 *See* Chapter 2, Section 2.2.3.

160 About JCIC, Joint Credit Info. Center, www.jcic.org.tw/main_en/docDetail.aspx?uid=242&pid=237&docid=347 (last visited Sep. 10, 2019) (hereinafter About JCIC).

161 *See* Yu, *supra* note 155.

162 *See id.* The board members and supervisors of the JCIC are assigned by the FSC, BAROC, and the Central Bank of the Republic of China (Taiwan) (the "CBC") or selected from scholars. JCIC, Annual Report 2018, at 10–11 (2018). Thus, it seems that the banking industry would influence the operation of the JCIC to such a degree that the governance organs of the JCIC are composed largely of people associated with banks. Moreover, JCIC was historically created in 1975 under the BAROC, which "decided in 1992 to donate all the operating surplus of JCIC and transform it into a non-profit foundation." About JCIC, *supra* note 160.

163 Yu, *supra* note 155.

164 Xing-Yi Guo (郭幸宜), *Jie Gui Jin Rong Ke Ji Ye Lian Zheng Zhong Xin Ni She Di Er Zi Liao Ku Yu Ji Ming Nian Di Shang Xian* (接軌金融科技業 聯徵中心擬設第二資料庫 預計明年底上線) [*Connecting the FinTech Industry, the JCIC Is Planning on Creating the Second Data Pool, Expected to Operate by the End of 2021.*], Ju Heng (鉅亨) [Anue], (Nov. 19, 2020), https://news.cnyes.com/news/id/4544087.

5 An Approach that Truly Promotes Financial Innovation, Competition, and Inclusion in the Era of FinTech

This chapter will propose a policy solution that truly promotes financial innovation, competition, and inclusion in the era of FinTech. Our solution comes from an institutional design perspective and is based on the findings in the previous chapters. Section 1 details this solution; Section 2 summarizes succinctly the OB regulatory background, Taiwan's problematic approach to OB regulation, and how our suggested solution addresses it.

1 Policy Implications of Fostering Open Banking in Taiwan and Beyond

1.1 Mandating Open Banking Might Be More Favorable

In Chapter 4, we identified and discussed potential pitfalls of the regulatory policies promoting OB in Taiwan. We appraised these pitfalls by comparing Taiwan's OB regulatory policies with those of the EU and the UK, where OB is mandated. Our aim was to draw policy implications therefrom while testing the lessons learned in the case study on Taiwan's voluntary OB reforms.

From a higher-level perspective, OB, as part of the FinTech revolution, has been trending in various jurisdictions thanks to its ability to encourage competition and empower consumers to give consent to share their own data stored in banks' data pools.[1] The UK's OB and EU's PSD2 reflect a compulsory pathway, emphasizing the importance of coercive mandates exercised by regulators in developing and implementing policies contributing to financial competition and innovation.[2] Through these OB models, regulator-led reforms, rather than deregulation on a voluntary basis, are adopted to promote innovation.[3] In the era of FinTech, these OB regulations epitomize a "pro-competitive paradigm" by mandating that information or data be accessible.[4] In this "pro-competitive paradigm," the role

DOI: 10.4324/9781003126324-5

of regulators was intentionally crafted so the regulators (and regulations) could help ensure that new players, such as FinTech startups, would be free from exploitation and regulatory capture could be avoided.[5] The UK's OB is regarded as a success as it permitted a large number of consumers to access alternative products and services, ultimately increasing financial competition and inclusion.[6]

Even so, a compulsory approach to OB is not always perfect. For instance, commentators argue that such a compulsory approach is inconsistent as it requires ASPSPs—mainly banks—to open their data pools, while AISPs and PISPs—mainly FinTech firms—are not required to reciprocally open theirs to banks.[7] Consequently, it may unintentionally lead to a competitive disadvantage for those who are required to open their data pools under regulations; or, worse, the compulsory approach may promote BigTechs' dominance as they might benefit from this approach due to the lack of reciprocity.[8] However, we cannot blame the promotion of BigTechs' dominance exclusively on the compulsory approach. Enhancing various market players' access to data in a common way, OB regulation per se brings benefits to BigTechs as they would more easily enter the financial industry.[9]

Similarly, a voluntary approach adopted by Taiwan has its own pros and cons. Specifically, it is doubtful whether banks are sufficiently incentivized to join this OB ecosystem and open their data pools to competitors. Low motivation of banks might eventually affect rate of participation by banks; this may signify a problem in a voluntary approach to OB regulation.[10] Moreover, the root causes of potential failures in Taiwanese OB policies seem to be closely associated with FSC's unwillingness to impose coercive mandates and the strong (and related) influence possessed by traditional banking industry, which makes it difficult to realize the goals of OB.[11] In addition, concerns about a voluntary approach are also reflected in Hong Kong and Singapore, which both adopt a voluntary approach to OB. In Hong Kong, for example, it was reported that the regulator had to nudge banks to open data and, still, the FinTech startups found it difficult to access data, as they were required "to provide a business case and negotiate with each and every bank to get access."[12] Meanwhile in Singapore, the lack of "standardization of the APIs . . . and common infrastructure and processes" created institutional barriers that FinTech startups could not overcome due to the time and money they would need to invest beforehand.[13] Similar concerns might be envisaged in Taiwan.

In fact, through the case study on the OB policies in Taiwan, we observed that its voluntary approach, that is, self-regulation rules established by banks themselves, might create a chance for legacy financial institutions to seek rents (from the perspective of economics) as the entry barriers facing, for example, FinTech startups would remain.[14] Furthermore, the regulator might be influenced more easily in the context of self-regulation at least in theory.[15] Our case study on the OB policies in Taiwan supports these notions. In Taiwan, OB reform is promoted through the self-regulations drafted by the BAROC, and FinTech-related policies have historically been intertwined with issues related to regulatory conservativeness or inertia.[16] It is consequently doubtful whether the benefits of OB could be unleashed effectively in Taiwan via the current voluntary and self-regulatory approach.[17] Therefore, mandating OB in Taiwan might be worthy of consideration as a regulatory solution to the long-standing problems that arise with FinTech development. Although, as mentioned earlier, a compulsory approach may result in different problems due to the lack of regulatory reciprocity, these problems are less concerning in Taiwan than they may be in a jurisdiction like China.[18]

1.2 Institutional Design of Financial Regulators in the Era of FinTech

A Taiwanese scholar noted that regulating FinTech may be difficult because of a regulator's limited resources, conflict of interests, or insufficient incentives for regulators to exercise internal controls.[19] Our study of Taiwan's OB self-regulation mirrored the aforementioned concerns, further showing that the influence of some interest groups aggravate difficulties in regulating FinTech as the regulation cannot realize public interest goals. On the other hand, the influence of the interest groups on regulation that renders regulation imperfect does not mean that regulation should be removed.[20] In effect, from the practitioners' perspective, limiting financial incumbents' influence is necessary in Taiwan to a certain extent. In particular, the Chairman of Taiwan FinTech Corporation pointed out that FinTech firms in Taiwan need to be able to develop without being asked by the FSC to collaborate with financial incumbents.[21] The question then turns to how can this influence be removed? Our answer is to re-design the role of financial regulators. Before we demonstrate how to establish an independent regulator that focuses on FinTech, we first explain why other potential alternatives would be less effective solutions.

One way to solve the aforementioned problems stemming from OB self-regulation, aside from emphasizing the role of the regulator, would be to facilitate bargaining between the self-regulatory bodies such as the BAROC and the intended beneficiary of the self-regulation such as FinTech startups.[22] Nevertheless, as shown by FinTech startups' experience in Hong Kong, such bargaining seems to be difficult or infeasible due to the high transaction costs.[23] Under such a model, the public agency in Hong Kong or Taiwan would need to serve a more significant role in order to oversee agreements of self-regulatory bargaining "to ensure that they are consistent with the statutory goals and, if necessary, [to] enforce[e] them."[24] Thus, rethinking the role of financial regulators from an institutional-design perspective might then be helpful in terms of developing OB in Taiwan. In fact, using this institutional-design approach for improving regulations in era of Fintech or digitalization has been successful in some instances.[25] Specifically, this organizational aspect seems favorable in Taiwan as the former FSC's chairman used to touch upon such a perspective when discussing how to reform the FSC in the era of FinTech.[26] Following this trend, rethinking "financial regulator" reform in the era of FinTech would be feasible. We suggest in particular that the ultimate goal of such reform is to promote financial innovation and competition in the age of FinTech. Accordingly, we argue that the regulatory design for FinTech should be well-crafted to support various goals such as enhancing financial inclusion as well as promoting financial innovation and competition.[27]

Based on the earlier discussion, we first suggest further involvement of public authorities by introducing an entity that has public nature. This entity should be familiar with the FinTech market in order to truly understand and facilitate it.[28] To enhance its independence, the entity should have some experience and expertise in FinTech.[29] The entity's composition would be important as well. Specifically, in order to fulfill its goals, the entity would require a professional staff to be responsible for achieving those goals.[30] In addition, ethical standards for those professionals within the entity should be set to avoid the influence of private interests.[31] Through the reforms and institutional-design, such an entity could facilitate information flow and improve access to data in the context of OB to not only fulfill its public interest goals but also to information-driven finance more broadly.[32]

The JCIC has served a comparable role in Taiwan.[33] However, due to the JCIC's vulnerability to be influenced by interest groups (i.e., the banking industry), it could not meet the requirements of the suggested public entity above—that is, being sufficiently independent so as to improve self-regulation.[34] Instead, due to the JCIC's lack of independence from the banking industry, the traditional financial institutions have long been at the root of some of the failures in FinTech regulations and policies in Taiwan.[35]

Therefore, we suggest a more fundamental or holistic solution from an institutional-design perspective, which is the creation of an independent regulator. With respect to the organizational arrangement, this regulator would be not susceptible to influence like traditional financial regulators.[36] Such an independent regulator would be beneficial not only because it might be less vulnerable to possible influence but also because it would have concentrated responsibilities instead of the mission conflicts currently haunting the FSC.[37] We will elaborate on this structural-design solution later.

1.3 Proposal for an Independent Regulator to Promote Financial Innovation, Competition, and Inclusion

1.3.1 Possible Candidates for the Independent Regulator that Would Resist the Influence of Potential Interest Groups

The creation of an independent and professional regulator that specializes in promoting financial competition, innovation, and inclusion might be helpful to effectively deliver the benefits of FinTech through OB.[38] Theoretically, the pressure from a single interest group may be arguably less significant when the regulator regulates multiple other interest groups; hence, a sole regulator with an array of powers is said to be more resistant to industry pressure.[39] In effect, the independence of this regulator helps not only resist the influence of interest groups but also adapt to the changes of the industry thanks to its expertise.[40] Meanwhile, our study of Taiwan's OB regulation showed something further. Specifically, the existence of conflicting missions of a sole regulator may, in theory, be dangerous due to "a significant risk that industry pressure and a focus on short-term economic concerns that are easily monitored will trump the long-term effects on the public that are harder to assess."[41] In practice, such a phenomenon has already been observed in Taiwan. One of the root problems with respect to FinTech-related policies in Taiwan is the conflicting responsibilities of the FSC, leading to the regulator's prioritizing its missions of prudential regulation (together with even consumer financial protection) at the expense of financial competition and innovation due to the potential to invite industry pressure.[42]

Accordingly, we propose—as a more fundamental strategy of regulatory intervention to enhance FinTech innovation, competition, and consumer welfare (or financial inclusion)—a specialized and independent regulator, which is similar to the UK's CMA, to alleviate the problems of mission conflicts.[43] The missions of promoting financial competition and innovation could be assigned to an existing entity such as the existing competition authority in Taiwan, the Fair Trade Commission (the FTC), and such an agency could be provided with a more powerful voice like the CMA.[44] By housing the financial competition and innovation bureau (FCIB) within the FTC, this new regulator would be positioned at the same hierarchical level as the FSC while being simultaneously independent of it. Specifically, since the independence of the FTC is stressed,[45] it might be a suitable candidate to play the role in promoting OB in particular or FinTech competition and innovation in general, to avoid the possibility that financial competition and innovation are "neglected due to co-location with stability regulation," as seen in the FSC's current configuration.[46] When promoting OB, the UK's experience in establishing the OBIE as a quasi-public regulator might be useful.[47] Further, rather than delegating to an SRO (such as the BAROC, which is composed all of incumbent financial institutions and prone to regulatory capture) the independent regulator's powers to implement OB policies, we suggest that structural control of such a quasi-public entity be transferred to the aforementioned independent regulator,[48] just as in the case of the OBIE controlled by the CMA.[49]

Another candidate for the independent regulator role is the "Ministry of Digital Affairs" (MDA) in Taiwan. The MDA, a newly established agency tasked with digital affairs possibly including finance, has been largely ignored, even while people's demand for digital financial services rises.[50] As reported, the establishment of the MDA was approved in December 2021, and the MDA commenced operations in 2022.[51] A commentator also argued that the MDA should be responsible for, among other tasks, developing innovation and helping the digital transformation in industry.[52] The government similarly announced in March 2021 that one of the three main areas on which the MDA will focus on is to accelerate the digital transformation of Taiwan.[53] Thus, if the MDA could be responsible for FinTech-related tasks, the goal of accelerating Taiwan's digital transformation would be better achieved. Assigning OB-related or, more generally, FinTech-related tasks to MDA also resonates with scholars' suggestion that a central government agency is more suitable for leading OB with its wider-level perspective.[54] However, as we will discuss later, coordination between governmental agencies would be critical to its success. The collaboration between the MDA and the existing financial regulator, which is the FSC, has also been emphasized by commentators.[55] Such collaboration is important when developing and regulating digital technology or FinTech.[56] This coordination concern is exemplified and noted during the process of establishing MDA as problems of coordinating opinions between authorities concerned used to disturb or dwarf its establishment.[57]

1.3.2 Organizational Arrangements of the Independent Regulator

1.3.2.1 THEORETIC INQUIRY

In theory, the success of housing the new independent agency lies, in part, in its accountability and the degree of independence.[58] Specifically, to what degree would it be susceptible to oversight and, therefore, external influences? How much independence should this regulator have? Or how could such a regulator gain this independence from an institutional-design perspective? These issues relate to organizational arrangement and the management of such an independent regulator, because careful and appropriate arrangement and management would be critical to the extent to which public interests are fulfilled.[59] To answer these questions, according to Ogus, forms of the regulators' accountability include the following: first, financial accountability (which is related to the financial standards that regulators should meet); second, procedural accountability (which emphasizes the due procedure adopted by regulators when making decisions); and third, substantive and structural accountability (which refers to the fact that decisions regulators make should be justified to facilitate adherence to goals public interests, as well as the structure or composition of the regulators in formulating policies to "serve the public interest and for resisting the undue influence of private interests").[60] In the following section, we discuss how scholars, such as Braithwaite and Selznick, emphasized the need of the regulator to listen to broader interests.[61] These arguments provide us insights into the institutional arrangements of the independent regulator we propose.

Further, the aforementioned financial and procedural controls could be ensured by principles of administrative laws or due process in a broader sense.[62] To ensure due process, the extent of a regulator's independence in terms of its procedural control should be subject to, for instance, fair hearings.[63] Similarly, guaranteeing participation rights of different private interest groups might at least "reduce inequalities in the power of pressure groups" when it comes to voicing their opinions.[64] Additionally, enforcing these participation rights would be beneficial as it would allow the participants the ability to provide information that rule makers or regulators need or should refer to.[65] Indeed, the success of our solution still turns on more detailed design to be envisioned in the future. We, however, point out that having such an independent financial regulator in the era of FinTech is indispensable and that the following conceptual framework based on the aforementioned theoretic inquiry would help ensure the independence and accountability of this regulator.

1.3.2.2 CONCEPTUAL FRAMEWORK

The presentation of a more detailed and complete solution to the problem of OB regulation in Taiwan would require additional research; therefore, we propose, on the basis of the preceding discussions, a conceptual framework that ensures the independence and accountability of this independent regulator. First of all, we suggest that FinTech companies should be guaranteed an opportunity to participate in the regulatory development as our case study shows that the lack of this specific participation inhibits the promotion of FinTech competition and innovation.[66] In the current regulatory model in Taiwan, the participation of such private actors such as incumbent banks seems to be overemphasized, which leads to possible regulatory failure if the banks' interests override those of FinTech firms.[67] Therefore, allowing a broader and more diverse group of stakeholders (including the disadvantaged or underprivileged groups like FinTech startups) to offer their insights and, then, secondarily, respecting those insights are both essential.[68] In other words, promoting FinTech startups' participation might alleviate the current over-reliance on the banking industry when formulating and implementing OB policies, thereby mitigating regulatory capture to a certain extent by "helping to equalize the influence of different interest groups."[69] As a commentator in Taiwan noted, the participation of FinTech firms in the financial market in Taiwan is evitable, yet financial regulation has been protecting financial institutions from being threatened by FinTech companies.[70] Thus, when building a financial ecosystem it is important to ensure that different players could enter the market fairly to serve consumers in this ecosystem.[71]

In addition to guaranteeing FinTech firms' participation, the regulatory process through which this independent regulator makes decisions should be enhanced.[72] With respect to the structural control, this regulator should be composed of professionals that are less prone to influence from private interest groups such as industry associations. Moreover, these professionals should be involved in the process through which this independent regulator makes decisions.[73] The participation of experts, illustrated earlier, would also contribute to the success of this independent regulator.[74] Furthermore, when complemented with the aforementioned financial accountability of the regulatory body, this independent regulator should be subject to external controls such as financial management assessments.[75] Specifically, given that regulations incur costs (a fact that some prior studies tend to forget or leave out),[76] there must be some limit to the independent regulator's authority such that costs, including, inter alia, compliance costs regulatees may encounter or the costs of establishing this independent regulator itself, are assessed, monitored, and tracked.[77]

Notwithstanding the forms in which such a specialized and independent regulator would be created, coordination and collaboration between the new regulator and the primary existing financial regulator, that is, the FSC, is necessary.[78] Specifically, as noted by a scholar in Taiwan, in the context of OB and data sharing, the method for clarifying the responsibilities among regulators is critically important as OB and data sharing involves various issues such as promoting competition and ensuring consumer protection.[79] In the case of Taiwan, housing the new regulator within, for instance, the FTC is beneficial as it generates "less mission conflict than prudential regulators" and "a coordinated antitrust approach across diverse markets" as markets turn "more intermediated and technological."[80] Even so, the coordination and collaboration between this new regulator and others should be ensured. In the UK's successful compulsory model, when it comes to OB regulation, the FCA and CMA communicate effectively, demonstrating the importance of such collaboration.[81] Similarly, in the case of regulating the sharing economy, some argue that "[t]he state could establish a separate sharing economy coordinating entity with representatives from each of the municipalities significantly affected by sharing transactions."[82] A commentator in the US, who used the Financial Stability Oversight Council (the FSOC) to demonstrate how interagency coordination plays an important role, indicated that "FSOC was designed for such an interagency oversight role, with voting representatives from diverse financial regulators—including the Federal Reserve, the SEC, and the CFPB" and contended that "[t]o guard against overenforcement by the new financial competition leader, FSOC might be tasked with vetoing financial competition actions with a two-thirds vote."[83] The commentaries here reiterate the importance of collaboration and coordination among multiple regulators.[84] By analogy in Taiwan, at least in the short term, we could propose assigning a "minister without portfolio"[85] in Taiwan's Cabinet to ensure the enforcement and coordination between regulators of "consumer protection, stability, and competition."[86] Either the FTC or MDA could be responsible for the aforementioned enforcement and coordination in the long term as discussed before. Given that the MDA was established and will be in operation soon to cope with the digital-technology-related tasks, the emphasis on the collaboration between the FSC and the MDA exemplifies the importance of such a collaboration.[87] Further, as suggested by Chun Chen, a former premier in Taiwan, such a new and specialized regulator and its staff should aim to keep abreast of changes in the era of FinTech so as to adapt to new business models therein.[88] Above all, when designing FinTech regulations, the ultimate goals of the regulations—the promotion of FinTech innovation and competition—should be at the forefront of the regulatory intent and implementation.

2. Concluding Remarks

Modern financial markets have witnessed digital transformations owing to the FinTech revolution that triggered the emergence of new market players who facilitate information flow. Those transformations have merited the attention of financial regulators across jurisdictions. The trend of adopting OB regulations illustrates government responses to the transformations in financial markets. Specifically, the introduction of OB through regulation has shown that while new market players have emerged thanks to their abilities to reduce transaction costs by facilitating the information flow, they face entry barriers to the markets. Therefore, OB regulation appears not only to unleash these informational advantages but also to help the new market players enter the markets by urging or encouraging incumbent banks to open the data pools to these new market players. Since the opening of data pools could be achieved by either demanding or encouraging incumbent banks to do so, two different approaches—the compulsory and voluntary approaches—are described and discussed in Chapter 2.

Then, in Chapter 3, we analyzed the EU's and UK's OB regulations, namely PSD2 and its transplant in the UK, since they both exemplify the compulsory approach. We focused on the role of regulators based on varying features of OB regulation and its implementation. Next, in Chapter 4, this book also examined the OB regulatory policies in Taiwan, where a voluntary approach is adopted. By comparing Taiwan's OB regulatory policies with the EU's and UK's counterparts, specifically by examining the roles played by the respective regulators, we found some pitfalls in Taiwan's regulations. That is, as OB is promoted through the self-regulation developed by incumbent banks, these banks have an over-reaching role in regulating OB. We found that OB may not be truly realized because those banks and FinTech startups are, to a certain extent, competitors in Taiwan. Incumbent banks may not have sufficient incentives to join OB and hence to open their data pools, demonstrating that banks' private interests in practice prevail over goals of advancing public interests, such as fostering financial innovation, competition, and inclusion, when OB is in the form of voluntary self-regulation. It is therefore doubtful that financial innovation and competition can be fostered in the shadow of banks' private interests. When taking these findings into consideration, this book offers a solution by demonstrating how an institutional design approach could address the limitation of sector regulators when promoting FinTech innovation and competition. Given that Taiwanese OB regulatory policies seem to fail to fulfill these public interest goals, this book suggests that the organizational arrangements of financial regulators be re-crafted.

The comparative assessment of the regulatory policies promoting OB across the UK, the EU, and Taiwan sheds light on these issues. The explanations for the potential regulatory failures in Taiwan relate to the regulatory trajectory of FinTech-related issues and the organizational design of the Taiwanese financial regulator, namely the FSC. In particular the FSC has been criticized for its regulatory conservativeness and inertia in terms of developing FinTech-related policies. In addition, the FSC's implementation of OB policies has been influenced by the incumbent banking industry. For example, the FSC relied on the BAROC to develop self-regulation to put OB into practice. As a result, the regulation required that the FinTech startups—that desire to be the TSPs and to join OB—are assessed, selected, and governed by the banks. As shown, barriers to joining OB are created in this type of regulatory approach that encourages banks to open data to competitors on a voluntary basis. An underlying factor for this regime's failure is that the FSC has been historically vulnerable to regulatory capture.

Taking into consideration the UK and EU mandatory approaches to OB, our study of OB reforms in Taiwan demonstrates why adequate institutional and regulatory design is necessary to maximize the promotion of financial innovation and competition. Accordingly, we propose that the regulations should concentrate explicitly on the missions of promoting financial innovation and competition via an independent regulator in Taiwan's executive branch, for example, the FTC or MDA. In addition, we contend that this new regulator should have a role similar to the UK's CMA. The new financial competition and innovation bureau under the aforementioned governmental agencies would specialize in promoting financial innovation and competition at the same hierarchical level as the FSC.

As for the lessons learned from the Taiwanese case study, we assert—from an institutional design perspective—that an independent regulator, not subject to the traditional financial regulator like the FSC in Taiwan, is necessary to promote OB or open APIs in particular as well as financial innovation and competition in general. The regulatory-design proposal could serve as a fundamental pathway to ensure innovation and competition is promoted in financial markets situated in jurisdictions sincerely intending to unlock benefits of digital financial transformations. The OB policies discussed in this book illustrate the institutional infrastructure to be developed for FinTech-enabled financial innovation and competition. Complemented by our proposed organizational-design solution, such public policies would be supported more effectively in a FinTech ecosystem that benefits from digital financial inclusion.

Notes

1 *See* Ben Regnard-Weinrabe & Jane Finlayson-Brown, *Adapting to a Changing Payments Landscape, in* FinTech: Law and Regulation 23, 47, 49 (Jelena Madir ed., Edward Elgar Publishing, 2nd ed., 2021) (https://doi.org/10.4337/9781800375956).
2 *See* Jane K. Winn, *Reengineering European Payment Law* 5 (June 30, 2019), https://ssrn.com/abstract=3412457 (arguing that "EU policy with regard to innovation and competition in payment systems is developed within a coordinated market economy policy framework . . . ."). *See also* Giuseppe Colangelo & Oscar Borgogno, *Regulating FinTech: From Legal Marketing to the Pro-Competitive Paradigm* 1 (Mar. 29, 2020), https://ssrn.com/abstract=3563447 (advocating for "the paradigm of procompetitive regulation underlying Open Banking projects in the EU, UK, Australia[,] and other jurisdictions as the true game-changer approach that can unlock the potential of FinTech innovation").
3 Winn, *supra* note 2, at 32. In fact, Professor Jane Winn opines that it might be too early to deem this top-down approach a success. *Id.* at 31.

4 Colangelo & Borgogno, *supra* note 2, 16–17.
5 *Id.* at 17.
6 *See* Barney Reynolds, *Shearman & Sterling Discusses How UK Banking Is Affecting Global FinTech*, The CLS Blue Sky Blog (Apr. 19, 2021), https://clsbluesky.law.columbia.edu/2021/04/19/shearman-sterling-discusses-how-uk-banking-is-affecting-global-fintech/.
7 Nydia Remolina, *Open Banking: Regulatory Challenges for a New Form of Financial Intermediation in a Data-Driven World* 46 (SMU Centre for AI & Data Governance Research Paper No. 2019/05, 2019), https://ssrn.com/abstract–3475019; Brad Carr, Daniel Pujazon, & Pablo Urbiola, *Reciprocity in Customer Data Sharing Frameworks* 2, 6 (July 2018), www.iif.com/portals/0/Files/private/32370132_reciprocity_in_customer_data_sharing_frameworks_20170730.pdf.
8 *Id.* at 2; Remolina, *supra* note 7, at 30.
9 *See* Pinar Ozcan & Markos Zachariadis, *Open Banking as a Catalyst for Industry Transformation: Lessons Learned from Implementing PSD2 in Europe* 11 (SWIFT Institute Working Paper, July 2021), https://ssrn.com/abstract=3984857.
10 *See* Chapter 4, Section 1.3; Annette Elisabeth Töller, *Voluntary Approaches to Regulation – Patterns, Causes, and Effects*, in *Handbook on the Politics of Regulation* 499, 506 (David Levi-Faur ed., Edward Elgar Publishing Limited, 2011) (https://doi.org/10.4337/9780857936110). For instance, the case of Taiwan shows that banks were not fully incentivized to join OB. Jing-Yuan Gao (高敬原), Kai Fang Yin Hang Di Er Jie Duan "Ke Hu Zi Liao Cha Xun," Shen Me Yuan Yin Rang Ge Da Hang Ku Chi Wei Shen Qing? (開放銀行第二階段「客戶資料查詢」，什麼原因讓各大行庫遲未申請？) [*Phase Two of Open Banking – Customers' Account Data: Why Haven't Banks Applied for Joining this Phase?*], Shu Wei Shi Dai (數位時代) [Business Next], (Aug. 5, 2020), www.bnext.com.tw/article/58730/open-banking-second-stage-challenge.
11 Remolina, *supra* note 7, at 46 (noting that "mandatory data sharing frameworks" such as open APIs are introduced to "allow customers to transfer their data from one firm to another, with the aim of promoting greater competition, facilitating innovation in data-based solutions and empowering customers with more control over their data").
12 Hakan Eroglu, *The Asia-Pacific Way of Open Banking Regulation*, Finextra (June 20, 2019), www.finextra.com/blogposting/17396/the-asia-pacific-way-of-open-banking-regulation; *FinTechs Worry H.K. Banks Impeding Open APIs*, DIGFIN (Mar. 21, 2019), www.digfingroup.com/hkapi/.
13 Eroglu, *supra* note 11. As reported, a FinTech startup in Singapore found it difficult to compete for a digital wholesale banking license as the markets are intertwined with the traditional banking industry. Yoolim Lee & Chanyaporn Chanjaroen, *Singapore FinTech Startup Abandons Plans Competing for Digital Banking License*, Bloomberg Technology (Nov. 5, 2019), www.bloomberg.com/news/articles/2019-11-05/rebranded-instarem-abandons-singapore-digital-banking-race.
14 *See* David T. Llewellyn, *Regulation of Retail Investment Services*, 15 Econ. Aff. 12, 13 (1995) (recognizing, from an economic perspective, that "self-regulatory agencies may effectively impose barriers to entry").
15 *See* Anthony I. Ogus, *Rethinking Self-Regulation*, 15 Oxford J. Legal Stud. 97, 98 (1995); Anthony I. Ogus, *Regulation: Legal Form and Economic Theory* 108–9 (Hart Publishing, 2004) (http://dx.doi.org/10.5040/9781472559647).

16 *See* Chapter 4, Section 3.1.

17 According to a commentator, the current OB policies in Taiwan will likely maintain the competitiveness of the traditional financial institutions facing FinTech startups temporarily. This commentator advocated for Taiwan to implement the compulsory regulations like the EU and UK in order to promote financial competition and innovation and be prepared for global competitors from abroad. *See* Kun-Zheng Lin (林坤正), *Lin Kun Zheng: Yin Hang Men Hu Dong Kai, Shen Fang Qing Bing Ru Guan!* (林坤正：銀行門戶洞開，慎防「清兵入關」!) [*Kun-Zheng Lin: The Troy Gate to Army Conquering Banks to Be Opened: Be Wary of "Trojan Horse"!*], Cai Xun (財訊) [Wealth Magazine], (Sep. 18, 2019), www.wealth.com.tw/home/articles/22295.

18 *See* Jon Frost, Leonardo Gambacorta, Yi Huang, Hyun Song Shin, & Pablo Zbinden, *BigTech and the Changing Structure of Financial Intermediation* 2 (BIS Working Papers No. 779, Apr. 2019), www.bis.org/publ/work779.pdf.

19 Yueh-Ping Yang (楊岳平), *Ren Gong Zhi Hui Shi Dai Xia De Jin Rong Jian Li Yi Ti—Yi Li Cai Ji Qi Ren Jian Li Wei Li* (人工智慧時代下的金融監理議題—以理財機器人監理為例) [*The Issue of Financial Supervision in the Era of Artificial Intelligence – A Case Study on Robot-Advisor*], *in* Fa Lü Si Wei Yu Zhi Du De Zhi Hui Zhuan Xing (法律思維與制度的智慧轉型) [Smart Transitions of Legal Thinking and Institutions] 467, 499 (Jian-Liang Li (李建良) ed., Yuan-Zhao Publishing (元照出版社), 2020).

20 *See* George A. Akerlof & Robert J. Shiller, *Phishing for Phools: The Economics of Manipulation and Deception* 145 (Princeton University Press, 2015) (https://doi.org/10.2307/j.ctvc777w8).

21 Bi-Fen Chen (陳碧芬), *5 Yin Su Dang Guan Jin Rong Ke Ji Nan Kua Bu* (5因素擋關 金融科技難跨步) [*5 Factors Create Difficulties in FinTech's Development.*], Zhong Shi Xin Wen Wang (中時新聞網) [China Times], (Aug. 25, 2021), www.chinatimes.com/newspapers/20210825000131-260202?chdtv.

22 Theoretically, bargaining between the self-regulatory bodies and the beneficiaries is the first solution to the problems of self-regulation. Ogus, *supra* note 15, at 109.

23 *See* Section 1.1.

24 Ogus, *supra* note 15, at 101.

25 As for examples on FinTech regulation from an institutional-design perspective, *see, for example*, Dan Awrey & Kristin van Zwieten, *The Shadow Payment System*, 43 J. Corp. L. 775, 808 (2018) (noting that the PSD2 exemplifies a regulatory approach to giving institutions within the shadow payment system "extremely wide latitude to design institutional features to protect customers and minimize potential systemic risks."). Another example is the proposal to make the Digital Markets Act in the EU more effective from the institutional-design perspective; it was recommended that enforcement powers be concentrated and responsibilities of regulatory authorities be clearly arranged and refined. *See* Giorgio Monti, *The Digital Markets Act – Institutional Design and Suggestions for Improvement* 17–18 (TILEC Discussion Paper No. 2021–04, 2021), https://ssrn.com/abstract=3797730.

26 *See* Yu-Ning Chang (張育寧), *"Tai Wan Shu Wei Jin Rong Tui Shou" Zhuan Fang Jin Guan Hui Zhu Wei Gu Li Xiong: Kai Fang Yin Hang Shi Zai Bi Xing, Jin Guan Hui Ben Shen Ye Yao Shu Wei Hua Zhuan Xing* (【台灣數位金融推手】專訪金管會主委顧立雄：開放銀行勢在必行，金管會本身也要數位化轉型) [*"The Driving Force Behind Taiwan's Digital*

Finance"—Interview with the FSC Chairman Wellington Koo: Open Banking is Imperative, and the FSC Should Be Digitalized, Too.], Ke Ji Bao Ju (科技報橘) [TechOrange], (May 12, 2020), https://buzzorange.com/techorange/2020/05/12/open-banking-digital-transformation/.

27 Dirk A. Zetzsche, Douglas W. Arner, & Ross P. Buckley, *Fintech Toolkit: Smart Regulatory and Market Approaches to Financial Technology Innovation* 19, 22 (Apr. 1, 2020), https://ssrn.com/abstract=3598142. The perspective of regulatory design was also determined, in the context of regulation and innovation, to alter the impact of the former on the latter. *See* Yafit Lev-Aretz & Katherine J. Strandburg, *Regulation and Innovation: Approaching Market Failure from Both Sides* 5 (Dec. 2019), https://ssrn.com/abstract=3462522. Additionally, properly designed regulation was deemed to be crucial in developing decentralized finance, which is related to OB as they both facilitate democratization of finance by introducing more players. *See* Douglas W. Arner & Ross P. Buckley, *Decentralized Finance* 1, 44, 46, 52 (2020), https://ssrn.com/abstract=3539194.

28 *See* Saule T. Omarova, *Dealing with Disruption: Emerging Approaches to Fin-Tech Regulation*, 61 Wash. U. J. L. & Pol'y 25, 35–36 (2020).

29 *See* Saule T. Omarova, *What Kind of Finance Should There Be?* 83 L. Contemp. Probl. 195, 211–12 (2020).

30 Russel Hardin, *Institutional Morality*, *in* The Theory of Institutional Design 126, 137 (Robert E. Goodin ed., 1996).

31 Peter L. Kahn, *Politics of Unregulation: Public Choice and Limits on Governments*, 75 Cornell L. Rev. 280, 287–88 (1990).

32 The creation of "a public agency which has sufficient information to make appropriate judgments and can therefore act as proxy for average consumers" might improve the self-regulatory policies by facilitating the information regarding quality or results of the self-regulation. *See* Ogus, *supra* note 15, at 110.

33 *See* You-Huan Chen (陳佑寰), *Kai Fang Yin Hang Da Shi Suo Qu, Wan Shan An Quan Cuo Shi Jiang Di Feng Xian* (開放銀行大勢所趨完善安全措施降低風險) [*Open Banking Is an Unstoppable Trend; Risks Could Be Lowered with Complete Safety Measures*], Wan Guan Ren (網管人) [NATADMIN], (July 10, 2019), www.netadmin.com.tw/netadmin/zh-tw/viewpoint/9F6D22BB76F54 B70A83E612B7306259A. Similar to the FISC, because the JCIC, which was albeit a private foundation nominally, has been assisting in implementing public policies, it appears to be a quasi-public entity or a private entity with public nature in practice. More elaboration on the nature of quasi-public entities, *see* Yueh-Ping Yang & Chen-Yun Tsang, *RegTech and the New Era of Financial Regulators: Envisaging More Public-Private-Partnership Models of Financial Regulators*, 21 U. Pa. J. Bus. L. 354, 403 (2018).

34 *See, for example,* Ogus, *supra* note 15, at 110–11 (highlighting that "[a]s a result of pressure brought to bear on politicians by practitioner groups during the legislative process, the membership of the second-tier agencies is sufficiently independent and is clearly vulnerable to capture by the incumbent monopolists") (footnote omitted).

35 *See* Chapter 4, Section 3.1.

36 *See* Rory Van Loo, *Making Innovation More Competitive: The Case of FinTech*, 65 UCLA L. Rev. 232, 275–78 (2018); Chang-Hsien Tsai, *To Regulate or Not to Regulate? A Comparison of Government Responses to Peer-to-Peer Lending among the United States, China, and Taiwan*, 87 U. Cin. L. Rev. 1077,

1120–22 (2019) [hereinafter *Peer-to-Peer Lending*, Tsai]; Chang-Hsien Tsai, *Choosing Among Authorities for Consumer Financial Protection in Taiwan*, *in* The Political Economy of Financial Regulation 219, 242–43 (Emilios Avgouleas & David C. Donald eds., Cambridge University Press, 2019) (http://doi. org/10.1017/9781108612821.009).

37 *See* Van Loo, *supra* note 36, at 242; *Peer-to-Peer Lending*, Tsai, *supra* note 36, at 1120.

38 *See* Rachel E. Barkow, *Insulating Agencies: Avoiding Capture Through Institutional Design*, 89 Tex. L. Rev. 15, 19 (2010) (noting that "[t]he main aim in creating an independent agency is to immunize it, to some extent, from political pressure," and that "[w]hat policy makers who seek insulation want to avoid are particular pitfalls of politicization, such as pressures that prioritize narrow short-term interests at the expense of long-term public welfare."); Cristie Ford, *Making Regulation Robust in the Innovation Era* 11 (May 2021), https://ssrn. com/abstract=3839865.

39 *See* Jonathan R. Macey, *Organizational Design and Political Control of Administrative Agencies*, 8 J. L. Econ. & Org. 93, 99–100 (1992); Barkow, *supra* note 38, at 50.

40 *See* Marver H. Bernstein, Regulating Business by Independent Commission 295 (Princeton University Press, 1955) (http://doi.org/10.1515/9781400878789); David A. Moss & Daniel Carpenter, *Conclusion: A Focus on Evidence and Prevention*, *in* Preventing Regulatory Capture: Special Interest Influence and How to Limit It 451, 455 (Daniel Carpenter & David A. Moss eds., Cambridge University Press, 2014) (https://doi.org/10.1017/CBO9781139565875.022).

41 *See id.*

42 *See* Chang-Hsien Tsai, Ching-Fu Lin, & Han-Wei Liu, *The Diffusion of the Sandbox Approach to Disruptive Innovation and Its Limitations*, 53 Cornell Int'l L. J. 261, 289–90. Taiwan's experience in applying the regulatory sandbox to FinTech also shows that the current approach, which is solely led by the FSC, might not be efficient. *See* Xiang-Yi Gu (古湘儀), *Cong Jie Kou Tuo Fu Bao Shi Jian Kan Wo Guo Jian Li Sha He Tiao Li Fa Zhan Cheng Xiao* (從街口託付寶事件 看我國監理沙盒條例發展成效) [*Examining the Efficiency of Our Regulatory Sandbox Act Based on the Case of JKOPAY*], Gong Shang Shi Bao (工商時報) [Commercial Times], (Sep. 14, 2020), https://view.ctee.com. tw/monetary/23096.html?amp.

43 *See* Oscar Borgogno & Giuseppe Colangelo, *Consumer Inertia and Competition-Sensitive Data Governance: The Case of Open Banking* 1, 11 (Jan. 3, 2020), https://ssrn.com/abstract=3513514.

44 *See* Chapter 3, Section 2.1.1. The Taiwanese FTC was established on January 27, 1992, in accordance with the Fair Trade Act, which was enacted and promulgated on February 4, 1991, with a focus on the enforcement of the Fair Trade Act and the formulation of relevant competition policies. *A Word from the Chairperson*, FTC, www.ftc.gov.tw/internet/english/doc/docDetail. aspx?uid=196&docid=232 (last visited Dec. 7, 2019). In particular, the independence of the FTC is emphasized. *Id.* Thus, it seems that the FTC is similar to the CMA in the UK when it comes to the emphasis on their role as a single and powerful regulatory body dealing with competition issues.

45 *Id.*

46 Van Loo, *supra* note 36, at 270. As previously discussed, sector regulators may be captured by the industry and tend to prioritize their primary tasks over

missions of promoting competition, and there might be lack of expertise with respect to competition issues. Samuel N. Weinstein, *Financial Regulation in the (Receding) Shadow of Antitrust*, 91 Temp. L. Rev. 447, 485 (2019). Thus, it seems that the FTC may be an adequate candidate among existing government agencies on which we would confer the authority to promote FinTech competition and innovation, because it is independent of the FSC which has stability mandate and equipped with expertise about competition issues. To be sure, this regulatory re-design to house a financial competition and innovation office within a generalist antitrust agency might have several drawbacks such as lack of financial-specific expertise in implementing "a tailored competition policy in the fintech era." Van Loo, *supra* note 36, at 270, 275–76. Its establishment also inevitably could incur various costs.

47 *See* Chapter 3, Section 2.1.1.

48 According to commentators, the delegation to quasi-public organizations with more public-interested–oriented operation might be favorable when it comes to financial-innovation-related public policies. Yang & Tsang, *supra* note 33, at 403.

49 *See* Chapter 3, Section 2.1.1.

50 Jia-Hua Ye (葉佳華), *KPMG He Ding Tai Wan Jin Rong Ke Ji Bai Pi Shu》 Yang Rui Fen Ti Chang: She Li Shu Wei Fa Zhan Bu* (KPMG核定台灣金融科技白皮書》楊瑞芬提倡：設立數位發展部) [*KPMG Published A White Paper on the FinTech in Taiwan; Rui-Fen Yang Suggested Establishing the Ministry of Digital Affairs*], Xin Chuan Mei (信傳媒) [cmedia], (Aug. 26, 2020), www.cmmedia.com.tw/home/articles/23107.

51 Yan-Ci Lu (呂晏慈), *Kuai Xun/Shu Wei Fa Zhan Bu Lai Le! Zui Kuai Ming Nian Gua Pai Li Yuan San Du Tong Guo Zu Zhi Fa* (快訊／《數位發展部》來了！最快明年Q1掛牌　立院三讀通過組織法 [*Breaking News/ The "the Ministry of Digital Affairs" Is Coming! With the Legislative Yuan Has Already Passed its Organization Act, this Ministry Will Be Operating as Soon as in Q1 Next Year.*], ETToday (Dec. 28, 2021), www.ettoday.net/news/20211228/2156049.htm.

52 Jing Ji Ri Bao (經濟日報), *Dui Shu Wei Fa Zhan Bu De Qi Xu* (對數位發展部的期許) [*Expectations for the Ministry of Digital Affairs*], Jing Ji Ri Bao (經濟日報) [Economy Daily News], (Apr. 15, 2021), https://money.udn.com/money/story/5628/5389035.

53 Jun-Hua Chen (陳俊華), *Xin She Shu Wei Fa Zhan Bu Zheng Wei: Gong Si Xie Li Chuan Cheng Zi An Guo Jia Dui* (新設數位發展部 政委：公私協力串成資安國家隊) [*Establishing the Ministry of Digital Affairs, a Minister without Portfolio Emphasizes Public-private Partnership to Create the National Information Security Team.*], CAN (中央通訊社) [CNA] (Mar. 25, 2021), www.cna.com.tw/news/aipl/202103250146.aspx.

54 Ross P. Buckley, Natalia Jevglevskaja, & Scott Farrell, *Australia's Data-Sharing Regime: Six Lessons for Europe* 35–36 (UNSW Law Research Paper No. 21–67, 2021), https://ssrn.com/abstract=3946668.

55 Lu, *supra* note 51.

56 *See id.*

57 Jing-Zhe Huang (黃敬哲), *Zheng Fu Nei Bu Yi Jian Bu Yi, Shu Wei Fa Zhan Bu Ji Cai Sha Che* (政府內部意見不一，數位發展部急踩煞車) [*Opinions Within the Government Are Conflicting So that Establishing of the Ministry of Digital Affairs Was Ceased.*], Ke Ji Xin Bao (科技新報) [TechNews], (Dec. 14, 2020), https://technews.tw/2020/12/14/

different-opinions-within-the-government-the-ministry-of-digital-development-stepped-on-the-brakes/.

58 *See* Ogus, *supra* note 15, at 117 (noting that "[p]articular institutions may be designated as regulators because their expertise and independence from political influence maximize the prospects of their fulfilling public interest goals," and that "[t]hose prospects are reduced if judgments may be overridden by other bodies which do not combine the degree of expertise and political independence").

59 *See* Steven J. Balla, *Institutional Design and the Management of Regulatory Governance*, in *Handbook on the Politics of Regulation* 70, 70 (David Levi-Faur ed., Edward Elgar Publishing Limited, 2011) (https://doi.org/10.4337/9780857936110).

60 Ogus, *supra* note 15, at 111.

61 *See* Section 1.3.2.2.

62 *See* Ogus, *supra* note 15, at 114.

63 *See id.*; Balla, *supra* note 59, at 72–73.

64 *See* Ogus, *supra* note 15, at 115.

65 Scott R. Furlong & Cornelius M. Kerwin, *Interest Group Participation in Rule Making: A Decade of Change*, 15 J. Public Adm. Res. Theory 353, 369 (2005).

66 *See, for example,* Chapter 4, Sections 2.1.6 and 3.2.

67 This phenomenon has been similarly discussed in literature. *See, for example,* Peter Grabosky, *Beyond Responsive Regulation: The Expanding Role of Non-state Actors in the Regulatory Process*, 7 Reg. & Gov. 114, 119 (2013); Neil Gunningham & Darren Sinclair, *Regulatory Pluralism: Designing Policy Mixes for Environmental Protection*, 21 Law & Pol'y 49, 50 (1999); Neil Gunningham & Mike D. Young, *Toward Optimal Environmental Policy: The Case of Biodiversity Conservation*, 24 Ecology L. Q. 243, 261–63 (1997).

68 John Braithwaite, *The Essence of Responsive Regulation*, 44 U.B.C.L. Rev. 475, 493 (2011); Philip Selznick, *The Moral Commonwealth: Social Theory and the Promise of Community* 465–66, 472 (University of California Press, 1994).

69 James Kwak, *Cultural Capture and the Financial Crisis*, in Preventing Regulatory Capture: Special Interest Influence and How to Limit It 71, 96 (Daniel Carpenter & David A. Moss eds., Cambridge University Press, 2014) (https://doi.org/10.1017/CBO9781139565875.008).

70 Jing Ji Ri Bao She Lun (經濟日報社論), *Zheng Shi Jin Rong Ke Ji Dui She Hui Jia Zhi Chong Ji* (正視金融科技對社會價值衝擊) [*Facing Squarely the Social Impacts Brought by FinTech.*], Lian He Xin Wen Wang (聯合新聞網) [UDN], (Sep. 12, 2021), https://udn.com/news/story/7338/5739938.

71 *Id.*

72 *See* Deniz O. Igan & Thomas Lambert, *Bank Lobbying: Regulatory Capture and beyond* 21 (IMF Working Paper No. 19/171, 2019), www.imf.org/-/media/Files/Publications/WP/2019/wpiea2019171-print-pdf.ashx.

73 *See* Ogus, *supra* note 15, at 113.

74 *See* Bernstein, *supra* note 40, at 282–83.

75 *Id.* at 113, 278.

76 Wim Marneffe & Lode Vereeck, *The Meaning of Regulatory Costs*, 32 Eur. J. L. & Econ. 341, 342 (2011).

77 Ogus, *supra* note 15, at 114, 162–65.

78 Remolina, *supra* note 7, at 3 (noting that "especially when choosing the in compulsory approach, coordination among different regulatory authorities is needed on a national and international levels . . . ."). In order to develop and enforce

policies or regulations in modern finance where legal issues might be more extensive or comprehensive than those which were traditionally conceived, coordination or collaboration among regulators is pivotal. *Id.* at 46–47. *See also* Verity Winship, *Enforcement Networks*, 37 Yale J. on Reg. 274, 277 (2020) (taking the SEC for example to indicate that "domestic and international agencies coordinate in civil investigation and enforcement").

79 Cheng-Yun Tsang (臧正運), *Tan Xun Zi Liao Shou Xin Zhe Zai Kai Fang Yin Hang Xia De Jian Li Zuo Biao* (探尋資料受信者在開放銀行下的監理座標) [*Exploring Regulatory Coordinates for Data Fiduciaries in the Era of Open Banking*], 23 Zhong Zheng Cai Jing Fa Xue (中正財經法學) [Chung Cheng Financial and Economic Law Review] 83, 109 (2020).

80 Van Loo, *supra* note 36, at 275.

81 *See* Chapter 3, Sections 2.1.1 and 2.1.2.

82 Janice C. Griffith, *The Sharing Economy: State and Local Regulatory Coordination Needed*, 42(2) St. & Loc. L. News. 8, 9 (2019).

83 Van Loo, *supra* note 36, at 277 (implying that understanding the behavior of the governmental agencies would help enhance the networks and coordination among different governmental agencies).

84 Winship, *supra* note 78, at 331.

85 *Executive Yuan Officials*, Executive Yuan, https://english.ey.gov.tw/Page/AD8E18A7B9608059 (last visited Aug. 28, 2020).

86 *See* Van Loo, *supra* note 36, at 278.

87 *See* Section 1.3.1.

88 Chun Chen (陳沖), *Dian Dong Che Zhi Hui Che Zhi Neng Jian Li* (電動車 智慧車 智能監理) [*Electric Cars, Smart Cars and Smart Regulation.*], Xin Shi Dai Jin Rong Ji Jin Hui (新世代金融基金會) [Appacus], (Nov. 5, 2021), www.appacus.org.tw/xmdoc/cont?xsmsid=0H255427663549293678&sid=0L309559888669372377.

Index

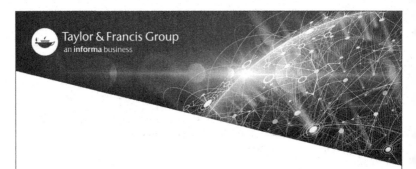

Printed in the United States
by Baker & Taylor Publisher Services